Vieques

A Photographically Illustrated Guide to the Island, Its History and Culture

Gerald Singer
Sombrero Publishing Co.

Copyright 2011by Gerald Singer
Sombrero Publishing Company
PO Box 1031
St. John VI 00831
Orders: www.SeeStJohn.com
All rights reserved. No part of this book
may be reproduced or transmitted in any form
or by any means, electronic or mechanical,
including photocopying, recording,
or by any information storage and retrieval system,
without written permission from the author, except
for the inclusion of brief quotations in a review.
Printed in China by Everbest
ISBN 978-0-9641220-9-3
Library of Congress Control Number: 2011908836
First Printing 2004
Second Printing 2006
Third Printing Revised 2011

Photo by Christine Aliberti

Acknowledgements

It is my wish to extend a heartfelt thank you to all the warm, wonderful and helpful people of Vieques and special gratitude to the following people without whose help this book would not have been possible:

Christine Aliberti, Bif Browning, Don Gabriel Carambot, Chepito of Chepito's Car Rental and Video Store, Carlos & Paulina Conde, Charlie Connelly & Myrna Pagán of *The Vieques Times*, Ura Connelly, Marc De Lucia and Erin Provost, Oscar Díaz, manager of the Vieques National Wildlife Refuge, Osvaldo Gonzalez of Vieques Air Link, Tato and Nelida Guadalupe, Elena Harley of Blue Heron Kayak Tours, Ramon Korff, Mark Martin of the Vieques Conservation & Historical Trust, Rosa Nevado, Robert Rabin, curator of the Museum Fort Count Mirasol, artist Sandra Reyes, Rosa and the staff of Taverna Española, Mario Solis Solis, Bob Tepper, Radames Tirado, former mayor of Vieques, Abe Velásquez of Abe's Snorkeling, Charlie Velásquez, Maria Velásquez of Monte Carmelo, Carlos (Prieto) Ventura and Carlos (Taso) and Aleida Zenón.

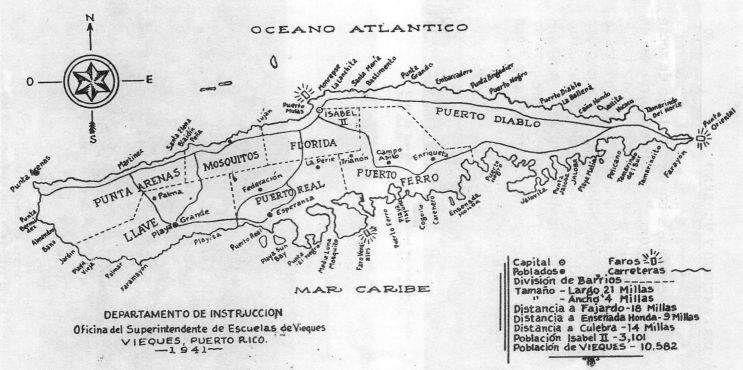

Mapa de la Isla de Vieques.
(Cortesía del Departamento de Instrucción - - Distrito escolar de Vieques)

Introduction

Vieques, A Photographically Illustrated Guide to the Island, Its History and Its Culture is not a guidebook in the traditional sense of the word. It does not contain practical information for the traveler, such as places to stay and where to eat. It does, however, endeavor to portray to the reader a more complete understanding of the island for those of you who, like me, are new to Vieques.

I try, through the media of photography, travel journal entries and stories told to me by residents, to impart a taste of the beauty and charming character of the island as well as an appreciation for the people and their heroic struggle for peace, justice and human dignity.

The fact is that Vieques is more than the stunning beauty of its magnificent landscapes, beaches, dramatic vistas, and charming town barely touched by modern global style development. Vieques is also an island with an often sad history, blotted by the abuses of centuries of colonialism and bearing the scars of more than 60 years of US Navy occupation during which the island and its people suffered injustices, insensitivity, economic and social hardships, and the destruction of much of its natural environment. For as beautiful and unspoiled as Vieques appears to the visitor of today, it is, unbelievable but true, a mere shadow of what it once was and what it hopefully can become again.

I have often heard the words "undeveloped, natural and unspoiled," used by travel writers and visitors to describe Vieques and I would like to put that into perspective.

With the US Navy using some three quarters of the land on Vieques as an ammunition dump and a bombing range, there was very little happening on the island in the free-for-all development days of the late twentieth century that effected so much of the Caribbean. Consequently, Vieques was able to maintain much of its original character and escape the onslaught (until now) of the results of unconstrained development such as traffic, congestion, fast food restaurant chains, global franchises, and sprawling condominiums and resorts dominating the beaches. The island also avoided much of the environmental and cultural consequences of irresponsible development. The price paid, however, was dear.

Over a half century of bombing, bulldozing and shelling have damaged or destroyed many of the coral reefs, mangrove lagoons and dry forests. The beach environments were negatively effected by the removal of vast coconut groves to facilitate war game practices. Worst of all, is the contamination left behind by the Navy in the form of heavy metals, depleted uranium, explosive residues, unexploded bombs and artillery shells and the dumping of toxic wastes.

Since the Navy has left Vieques, the island has been "discovered" for the third time: First by the indigenous peoples coming from the mainland of South and Central America, second by Christopher Columbus and the Europeans who followed him and presently by waves of tourists, speculators and developers. Consequently, the people of Vieques now face many difficult challenges that will determine the future course of the island.

The intention of this book is to impart our impressions of the awesome beauty of Vieques, to present you with images of the island that you can share with others, to guide you to those hidden and remote places often missed and to give you a sense of the history of the places that you will visit while, at the same time providing you with a sensitivity and respect for the warm, lively and friendly people who call Vieques their home.

Photo Courtesy of the US Department of Fish & Wildlife

The island of Vieques is a municipality of Puerto Rico located about seven miles east of the main island.

It has an area of 52 Square Miles and is approximately 21 miles long and four miles wide. The highest elevation is atop Mount Pirata at 1000 feet. The average temperature is 80° F. The population is approximately 9,300.

There are two towns, Isabel Segunda on the north, which is the administrative center and Esperanza on the south, which the tourism and entertainment center.

The name, Vieques, comes from the Taino word Bieque, meaning small land. The British called it Crab Island and it appears with that name on old English maps. Locally, Vieques is often affectionately referred to as *la isla nena,* or the little girl island.

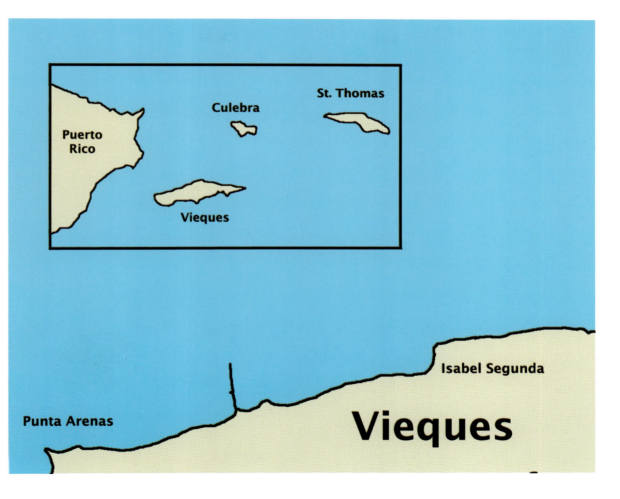

Table of Contents

El Norte - The North..................13
Isabel Segunda..................15
Colonial History..................33
Fortín Conde de Mirasol..................36
Festival Cultural Viequense..................40
Transportation..................44
Don Gabriel Carambot..................46
The Bees of Monte Carmello..................48
Horses of Vieques..................53
Playa Cofí..................57
La Lanchita..................59

El Oeste - The West..................63
Airport..................67
Osvaldo Gonzalez..................70
W Hotel..................73
Ceiba Tree..................76
La Peña..................77
Mosquito Pier (Rompeolas)..................78
US Takeover..................79
Victoria the Manta Ray..................83
Expropriation..................86
La Capilla Ecuménica..................89
Laguna Kiani..................93
Magazines..................95
Playa Grande..................99
Sugar..................100
ROTHR..................103
Punta Arenas..................104
Southwestern Beaches..................108

El Sur - The South..................113
Esperanza..................115
The Vieques Conservation and Historical Trust..................123
Ángel Rodríguez Cristóbal..................124
Sun Bay..................127
Mother's Day Battle at Sun Bay..................131
Cayo de Tierra..................132
Media Luna..................137
Navío Beach..................141
Bioluminescent Bay..................147
Playa Negra..................153
Fishing..................155
Puerto Ferro Man..................161
Cacimar and Yaureibo..................162

El Este - The East..................165
Eastern Lands..................166
Benefits of Navy Presence..................167
Wildlife Preserve..................168
Navy Out, Wildlife In..................169
Puerto Diablo..................173
Naming Vieques Beaches..................175
Playa Caracas..................176
Manuelquí..................179
Playuela..................183
Fishermen's War..................185
Civil Disobedience Camps..................189
Coconuts..................194
Community Activists Demands..................197
Bibliography..................199

El Norte - The North

Isabel Segunda

Isabel Segunda is considered to be the capitol of Vieques and houses the government offices. The town was founded in 1843, the same year that Queen Isabel II began her reign.

The Plaza

The Plaza or Public Square in Isabel Segunda was built around 1860 as a town cistern.

The concrete work for the plaza and the gazebo was a public works project of the Municipal Government in 1924. It was built using a system called *prestación*. Workers were required to give one day a week for public works projects. Those who didn't want to work had to hire someone else to take their place.

The photo on the right shows the plaza, which was renovated in 2008. At left is a photo of the plaza taken in 2003.

Bar Plaza

The Bar Plaza on the corner is the oldest bar on Vieques featuring a pool table and an antique jukebox.

Built in 1903, the structure was originally a pharmacy and later served as the post office until its next incarnation as the popular Bar Plaza.

In April of 2011, the Bar Plaza was severely damaged in a fire, but hopefully this landmark establishment will be restored and back in business soon.

The Catholic Church

The original Catholic Church, which stood in the same location, was a rustic structure covered by palm fronds.

On January 16, 1844, the first baptism was conducted and the first wedding was performed two days later.

A more permanent church was completed in 1860, in which year Bishop Pablo Benigno Carrión of Malagá, Spain came to Vieques where he performed 1,019 confirmations.

The Bishop died in 1871, when his coach overturned on the road between Fajardo and Luquillo on the Big Island.

The historical archives of Vieques, now residing at the Fort, were once kept in the Church.

For most of Vieques' history, this was the only church on the island, making it a social as well as a religious center.

The Episcopal Church

In the latter part of the nineteenth century many workers from the English colonies in the Caribbean came to Vieques to work in the burgeoning sugarcane industry. They came from the English colonies such as Nevis, St. Kitts, Anguilla, Antigua, Tortola, Virgin Gorda and Jost Van Dyke, and from the Danish colonies of St. Thomas, St. John and St. Croix. Most spoke English and attended the Episcopal Church.

In 1870, the Spanish Crown gave their permission to open a school in Vieques for children of the Protestant faith with classes to be conducted in English.

This was the first official incidence of religious tolerance in Puerto Rico and possibly in any of the territories under Spanish domination.

In 1880, Joseph Nathaniel Bean, known simply as Mr. Bean, came to Vieques. Mr. Bean was born in Bermuda and was of African decent. He was working on the small island of Jost Van Dyke in the Virgin Islands, when he heard that Vieques, where so many British Virgin Islanders had gone to work, had no Episcopal Church.

Through the efforts of Mr. Bean and the English workers on Vieques, the All Saints Episcopal Church of Vieques came into being.

Mass was given in English, until the demise of the sugar industry on the island, when most of the English-speaking parishioners left Vieques. Today, Mass is given in Spanish.

The original church was made of wood and it lasted until 1932, when it was destroyed by a hurricane. The church was rebuilt in concrete and exists to this day.

In the interior of the Church is an altar with paintings by artist, Terrence Price.

If you visit the church, look carefully at the painting to the right of the altar, and see if you can find the error in the painting.

Mambiche

The bridge found at the entrance to Isabel Segunda is known as Mambiche. The name was derived from a corruption of English into Spanish, when North American contractors were building what they called the "Main Bridge."

Mambiche

Masonic Lodge

The Masonic Lodge was built in 1902. This Lodge was named Union y Trabajo and it is situated on Calle San José across the street from the rectory of the Episcopal Church.

The Masons first established a presence on Vieques in the latter part of the 19th Century when Vieques was under Spanish rule. The first lodge was on Calle Le Brun and was called Alliance.

From the balcony of the lodge, there is a magnificent view of the town, the port, the north coast of Vieques, and the island of Culebra and its outlying cays.

Germán Rieckehoff School

The building shown in this photo taken in 2003 has recently been renovated. Originally a private residence, the owners donated it to the municipality and for many years it served as the public high school. The school was named in honor of Germán Rieckehoff considered to have been the most influential president of the Puerto Rican Olympic Committee.

The Movies

Presently there is no movie theater on Vieques, but back in the 1950s, there was a theater located right off the public plaza in the building where the gymnasium now stands. The "Teatro Nayda" would present Spanish language films from Hollywood, Mexico and Argentina.

On the nights when they where showing movies, people would congregate at the plaza before show time.

In those days, the young women wore ankle-length dresses called cancanes made with layers of crinoline petticoats that held the skirt up and out so that the ruffles bounced and swayed coquettishly. The style was provocative for the years of the 1950s because sometimes, if her movements were just right, an interested young man might be fortunate enough to catch a glimpse of the young lady's knees.

The young women would stroll around the plaza in one direction in groups of twos, threes and fours. Meanwhile, the young gentlemen of the town would ride their paso fino horses around the plaza, circling the square in the opposite direction. Giving each other the eye, they would flirting silently, while the older people would sit on the benches, chatting with each other and acting as the chaperones for the evening.

Photo by J. Lucas

Punta Mulas Lighthouse

The Punta Mulas Lighthouse marks the entrance to the harbor at Isabel Segunda. Constructed by Don Juan Puig Cerber in 1895, the Punta Mulas Lighthouse was the second lighthouse built on Vieques after the Faro Verdiales at the entrance to Puerto Ferro on the south coast.

The lighthouse serves to guide vessels approaching Isabel Segunda, an area surrounded by a chain of dangerous reefs lying off the north coast of the island. The red light from the tower can be seen from as far away as St. Croix and St. Thomas.

The lighthouse was restored and reopened on October 12, 1992 to coincide with the 500-year anniversary of Columbus' voyage to the Americas.

A museum inside features the maritime history of Vieques and the Americas as well as other historical and cultural exhibits.

The annex on the side of the lighthouse is available for public functions such as weddings and other gatherings.

"The hill where the lighthouse was built is called Punta Mulas by fishermen and navigators, but is known to the people of the town as Morropó. This name is a corruption of the French, *mon repose*. The story goes that a Frenchman had built a house on this hill, which he dedicated to rest and relaxation and because of this he named it, *Mon Repose*, (My Rest).

"The Frenchman went to this house every afternoon to relax and when the coachman would ask, 'Where can I take you?' He would answer, 'to *Mon Repose*.' The house has since fallen down and has disappeared completely, but the people continue to call the area in its Spanish form, Morropó"
Translated from *Vieques Antiguo y Moderno* by J. Pastor Ruiz, 1947

Colonial History

When the Spanish discovered the Americas, they conquered and colonized the largest and richest islands of the Caribbean, first Hispaniola, then Puerto Rico, Cuba and Jamaica, but they did not attempt to colonize the smaller islands.

Nonetheless, they claimed these islands for themselves, declaring that the entire New World was theirs and theirs only and that no other European country could come in and take over any of their self proclaimed territory.

Spain, however, lacked the wherewithal to enforce this audacious demand. Little by little, other European powers established bases in the Caribbean. England took over Jamaica and France took Haiti.

England, France, and Holland fought among themselves over the islands of the Lesser Antilles and the British and the Danes locked horns over the Virgin Islands. Meanwhile, Spain held tight to Puerto Rico, Santo Domingo and Cuba.

Vieques and Culebra, like most of the Caribbean Islands, were claimed by Spain, but not colonized. Lacking the wealth and potential of the larger islands, Vieques and Culebra were generally ignored by the Spanish in nearby Puerto Rico who referred to these lands as the *Las Islas Inútiles* or in English "the Useless Islands."

Although generally ignored by Spain, Vieques was not uninhabited. Fugitive Tainos from the Greater Antilles and Caribs from the Lesser Antilles hid out there. Pirates, privateers and buccaneers used Vieques as a base as did bands of fishermen, woodcutters, escaped slaves, deserters and wanted criminals. Small farms and some businesses were established and life went on.

Taking advantage of Spanish neglect and the proximity of Vieques to the British controlled Virgin Islands, England made several attempts to establish colonies on Vieques.

This was unacceptable to the Spanish, because although Vieques had little economic value compared to Puerto Rico, it did have strategic value. From Vieques you could see the movements of ships heading to Puerto Rico from the Lesser Antilles or the Virgin Islands. Also, a strong foreign power on Vieques could use the island as a base to attack Puerto Rico.

It was this strategic importance of Vieques, more than anything else, that was to determine its future.

Officially discovered by Columbus on November 19, 1493, Vieques was first explored by Europeans in 1524. The first settlers were French, but they were replaced by the English in 1666, who in turn, were expelled by the Spanish in 1688.

In the early 1700s, England began another attempt to establish themselves on Vieques. In 1718, Spain sent 300 soldiers on three warships to Vieques to drive out the English. The fort that the English had constructed was destroyed, the town burned, as were the fields of corn, cotton, sugar and tobacco. The colonists were taken prisoner, and the cannons from the English fort were carried to Puerto Rico and installed in the Castillo de San Gerónimo.

A few decades later, English settlers came back to Vieques and again began a settlement. In response, Spanish authorities in Puerto Rico sent another military expedition to Vieques in 1752. The English were subsequently defeated, their houses burned and their farms destroyed. The survivors were taken prisoner and their ships were captured, brought to San Juan and sold.

In 1811, the governor of Puerto Rico in an attempt to stabilize their position as far as Vieques was concerned, sent a Frenchman by the name of Roselló to be the military commandant there.

Roselló however, was ineffectual as commandant and Vieques remained in a state of anarchy, with a terrified Roselló hiding out in his country house where he more often than not could be found in a state of inebriation.

In 1823, the Frenchman, Le Guillou came to Vieques. He was the prosperous owner of a large sugar plantation in Haiti, but was forced to leave as a result of the slave rebellions.

Le Guillou had remembered Vieques from the days when he used to send men there to get hardwood for his piano keys. He had heard that Vieques was basically in a state of anarchy and guessed that the powers that be would welcome any chance for stabilization.

Le Guillou sailed to Puerto Rico and cut a deal with the governor of Puerto Rico in which he promised to establish a secure Spanish colony on Vieques in return for personal consideration from the Spanish government.

The deal made, Le Guillou sailed to the French Island of Guadeloupe and recruited a band of thugs who he armed to the teeth. They sailed back to Vieques and subdued the lawless inhabitants. Le Guillou established sugar plantations, which were, at the time, the most prosperous industries in the Caribbean.

Vieques was secured as a Spanish colony. Slaves were brought in by prosperous French immigrants from other Caribbean islands, notably the French colonies of Martinique and Guadeloupe. Discouraged by slave rebellions at home, they sold their holdings and established plantations on Vieques and the age of a sugar monoculture on Vieques began.

Simon Bolivar

Simon Bolivar arrived in Vieques on August 5, 1816. He is known in Latin America as the Great Liberator, having fought for the independence of the Spanish colonies in the Americas as well as for an end to the institution of slavery.

A bust of Simon Bolivar stands in the plaza in Isabel Segunda, honoring the first and only time that the Great Liberator set foot on Puerto Rican territory.

Bolivar had set out from Venezuela in July of 1816, where he fought for the independence of that land.

His army defeated, Bolivar and his surviving soldiers managed to escape on two ships, bringing with them refugees from the war, mostly women, children and elders. His plan was to take them to the Danish controlled island of St. Thomas where they would be safe.

Bolivar was in desperate straights as he sailed past Puerto Rico. His ships were without food or water, he had no money and he and his men were demoralized by their recent defeat.

During the night, the ship carrying Bolivar struck Roca Quebrada off the coast of Vieques and went aground. In the morning, a Spanish warship approached the disabled vessel.

The captain and a party of soldiers came aboard Bolivar's ship to inspect his papers. Once aboard, Bolivar's men, an international collection of war-seasoned veterans subdued the boarding party.

In exchange for their lives, the captain agreed to transport the refugees to St. Thomas and to help Bolivar get his ship off the reef. This being accomplished, Bolivar led a party of men ashore on Vieques to gather provisions.

According to a complaint by Juan Roselló who held the title of Commandant:

> About eight o'clock at night, while in my house, which lies about one mile from the beach, I was taken by surprise by a band of insurgents. There were 35-40 of them including Venezuelans, Italians, French, Indians and even four Spaniards. They killed four bulls and all the chickens. They stole two barrels of salt, a barrel and a half of wheat, a trunk with clothing, papers and 186 pesos. They took an axe, tools, a rifle and two pistols and ransacked the house leaving it uninhabitable.
>
> The expedition was made up of a brigantine, a schooner and three small boats. According to the reports of several citizens of the island, the ships contained 300 armed men, 150 women and a good deal of artillery. And that aboard the brigantine was the famous Simon Bolivar…

El Fortín Conde de Mirasol (Count of Mirasol Fort)

The Fortín Conde de Mirasol is the cultural center of Vieques. It is where the historical archives of the island are now stored and is the location of the Vieques Museum of Art and History. In 1977, the fort was listed on the National Register of Historic Places.

For those interested in indigenous cultures, the Fort Museum features one of the best archeological collections of prehistoric artifacts in the Caribbean documenting the history and way of life of the original inhabitants of Vieques. There are also exhibits from the era of the Spanish colonization, the sugar years and the epoch of the United States Naval occupation.

Exhibitions of artwork, poetry photography and sculpture are also featured from time to time at the fort..

The Fortín Conde de Mirasol has the distinction of being the last fort ever built by the Spanish. The construction began around 1845 by the order of the Count of Mirasol, don Rafael Aristegui y Velez, then the Governor of Puerto Rico. The project, which took longer and cost much more than was originally estimated, took more than ten years to complete. The cost overruns were so great that Queen Isabel II, upon being asked time and time again for more money, was heard to question "if the walls of the fort were made of gold."

The Fort was equipped with cannons and housed the island's militia. Its presence served to consolidate Spanish control over Vieques, dissuading the British, French, Dutch and Danes from their attempts to establish colonies on the island and served to protect the Viequenses from raids by pirates and privateers. It was also the island's jail and was sometimes referred to as "La Disciplinaria."

Around 1900, the United States government, then in control of Vieques, installed a seismographic station at the fort. The North Americans used the fort primarily as a jail until the 1940s when the fort was abandoned and fell into disrepair. Several attempts were made to restore and paint the fort but even these projects were underfunded and no real progress was made until a campaign by the Yaureibo Cultural Center of Vieques pressured the Puerto Rican Institute of Culture to begin a restoration in 1989, which was completed in 1991.

Outside the fort you can enjoy the lovely landscaped grounds and spectacular views from the walled hilltop. A small shop on the main floor of the Fort has an extensive collection of books about Vieques and Puerto Rico. The shop also offers crafts, music and souvenirs. Admission to the Fort Museum is free, but donations are encouraged. The curator, Robert Rabin, as well as the staff of the museum are extremely knowledgeable and will be glad to answer any questions you may have.

The Fort Museum is opened to the public from Wednesday to Sunday between 10:00 A.M. and 4:00 P.M.

Photo by Steve Simonsen

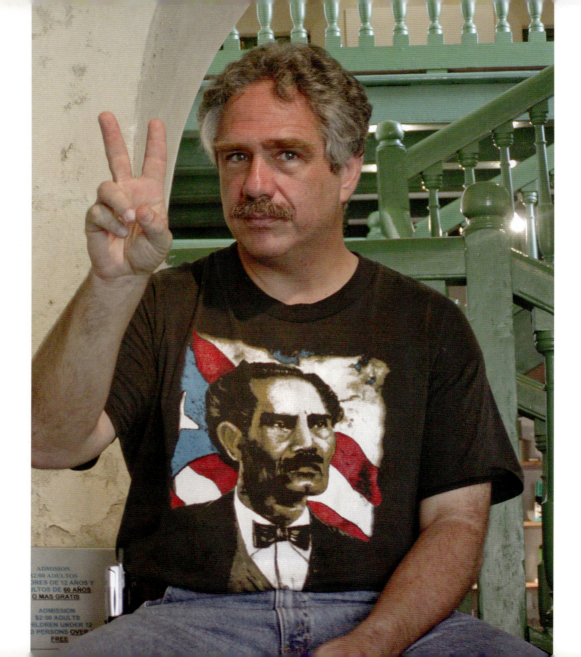

Roberto Rabin 2003

Vieques Cultural Festival

The thirty-fourth Vieques Cultural Festival was celebrated on the fifteenth through the seventeenth of April 2011 at the Museo Fuerte Conde de Mirasol. Ferries transported passengers from the island of Culebra and from Farardo on the Big Island to Vieques for the gala event.

In addition to various artistic, musical, and educational activities, a puppet show, book fair and folkloric musicians and dancers, the highlight of the festival was the free, open air performance of the Puerto Rico Symphony Orchestra appearing on Vieques for the first time in 50 years.

Públicos

Públicos or public taxis operate out of the airport and the ferry terminal. Fares are regulated by the government and range from $3.00 to $5.00 per person. You can also arrange to be picked up at a specific time and place or make other arrangements for an additional fee.

La Lancha (The Ferry)
The ferry travels between Isabel Segunda in Vieques and Fajardo on the Big Island. The trip takes a little over an hour and costs $2.00.

Don Gabriel Carambot

The painting by Sandra Reyes depicts Vieques' renowned healer, Don Gabriel treating a young boy. Introduced to the art by his uncle, Don Gabriel had been healing since he was 14 years old.

Don Gabriel passed away in 2004 just short of his 100th birthday. The street where he lived has been renamed in his honor.

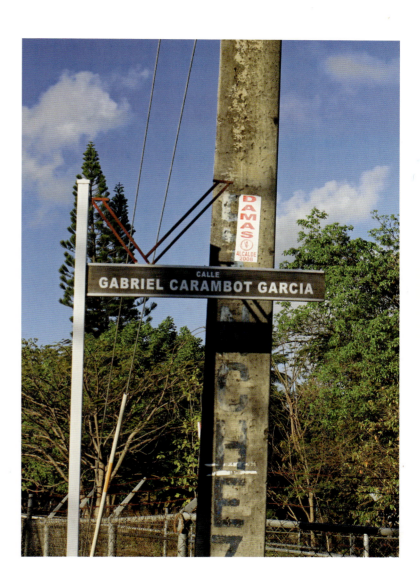

The Bees of Monte Carmelo

During the 1940s and 1950s, the US Navy expropriated three quarters of the privately held lands on Vieques. They fenced off this land and used it for an ammunition dump on the west side of the island and for a bombing range on the east. In addition, they claimed ownership to large tracts of land adjacent to these fences that were unused and unmarked. The exact limits and boundaries of these parcels, which the Navy called buffer zones, were ambiguous.

People living in crowded resettlement camps began to build homes, unopposed by the Navy or anyone else, on these spacious empty fields. Such was the case of a tract of land today known as Monte Carmelo.

Carmelo Felix, his wife Maria Velásquez and their family decided to build a home on top of a hill just to the west of the Navy range.

They cut a mile-long rugged road up the steep hill, brought in construction materials as best they could and made do without normal government supplied facilities such as water or electricity. They raised their family, planted trees and a garden, kept animals and cultivated honeybees.

There the family lived for several years undisturbed, until one day four Federal Marshals arrived from San Juan. They had come to Vieques to evict the Carmelos, claiming that they were trespassing on what was claimed to be Navy land.

In San Juan an eviction goes like this: The Marshals arrive, serve the evictees with papers from the court, and if they don't leave on their own accord, the Marshals will remove all their personal effects from the residence and deposit them at the nearest public area, usually the street in front of the house. The residents will then be forced from the premises and they will have to scramble to take care of their belongings.

But the Marshals found a different situation when they came to the home of Carmelo and Maria.

The family refused to move out of their home, claiming that the Navy had no right to the land, hadn't identified it and that there were no signs, fences or other indications that the land upon which their humble house sat belonged to the United States Navy.

As was mentioned before, the Felix home was at the end of a very rough mile-long dirt road beginning at the public highway below. The Navy was claiming that all land east of the highway was theirs, so that would make the nearest public area some distance from the house. It would be impossible for the four Marshals, without a proper vehicle, to effect the eviction in the usual way, that is, they couldn't carry all the stuff on foot, down the hill by themselves.

So the Marshals served the papers, got into their vehicle and went down the road to the Navy headquarters to explain the situation.

Meanwhile, the community at large became aware of the Felix family's problem. Friends, family and supporters began to arrive at the Felix home by the carload.

Back at Navy headquarters, Navy brass recruited a group of five enlisted men, who apparently were in the middle of a basketball game, to help the Marshals with the eviction. They also put at the disposal of the Marshals a flatbed truck with side panels and a smaller panel truck. In addition, telephone calls were made to Roosevelt Roads Navy Base in Ceiba, to the US Marshals' headquarters in San Juan and to the Vieques Police Department.

When all the pieces were in place, the four original federal Marshals, armed and in uniform, joined by a higher up from the Marshals' Office and the Judge Advocate General (JAG) from Roosevelt Roads in San Juan both wearing suits and ties and the five unarmed enlisted men wearing their basketball shorts and T-shirts, made their way up to the top of Monte Carmelo with the two vehicles.

They were jeered by the crowd that had gathered and was continuing to gather around the Felix home.

The Vieques Police Department, to their great relief, citing lack of jurisdiction on what was now said to be federal property, refused to participate in the eviction.

The Marshals came to the door once again, read their papers demanding that the Felixes leave the premises, and upon receiving a negative response from Carmelo, entered the home. Inside were four generations of the Felix family, from great grandmothers to kids to babes in arms.

The Marshals and Navy men started loading up the family's belongings bringing them to the truck parked outside, where they were booed and insulted by the crowd. After the heavy stuff like the furniture that Maria had just bought and hadn't paid for yet was loaded, the Navy team loaded smaller items onto bed sheets and carried them to the truck all the while trying to ignore the tears of the women and children and the consternation of the grandparents and the family.

The panel truck could be seen filling up with chairs and tables, baby cribs and beds, lamps and kitchen stuff, Bibles, books and the new set of encyclopedias, also not paid for.

At some point, someone, no one knows who or at least no one is telling, possibly one of the children, brought two boxes of bees into the house. A box of bees contains one total beehive with approximately 35,000 bees. The boxes are meant to be handled gently so as not to upset the bees.

Through signals, through communications in Spanish, a language that the Marshals did not readily understand and through just a general cultural knowledge of bees and boxes of bees, the Viequenses quietly and without a fuss left the house and went outdoors.

One of the Navy enlisted men in his shorts and T-shirt hefted up one of the boxes and threw it to the next man in line who passed it to the third man. Then the second box was picked up and unceremoniously thrown. The bees did not react for the first 30 or so seconds, but then they did. Seventy thousand angry bees swarmed the Navy men who ran for the door and the road swatting at the bees that were stinging them as they retreated. The Viequenses remained calm and stayed still knowing that bees rarely sting you if you remain motionless.

At this juncture, the Chief Marshal in the suit decided it was time to call it a day and bring the trucks and the accumulated stuff down the hill. The flatbed was parked nose to nose with the panel truck and needed to be

backed up before being able to access the driveway. As he ordered his men to get into the truck and take it away, Carmelo jumped under the rear wheels of the truck and started screaming that they would have to run him over and kill him before he would allow them to drive away carrying his family's belongings.

In the midst of all this confusion, jeering crowds, swarming bees chasing Navy sailors, and Carmelo screaming like a madman, someone noticed that smoke was coming out of the panel truck. It was on fire. (How the fire started or who started it is not known. A video tape taken by one of the bystanders, however, shows one of the men in suits lighting a cigarette and then entering the panel truck just minutes before the fire started.)

Carmelo came out from under the wheels and shouted to the Marshals to move the flatbed away from the panel truck before it too caught fire. "No one touches that truck," was the response and within minutes it too went up in a blaze of fire and smoke that could be seen from most of the island.

More people came to see what was happening. The Navy officer radioed for help and soon a Navy SWAT team armed with automatic weapons came up to Monte Carmelo to escort the Marshals and Navy men back to the base.

The Marshals declared the eviction to be completed and order restored.

The Felixes returned to their home, and with the help of friends, family and neighbors they were able to get back on their feet. Carmelo and Maria, their kids and their grandkids live to this day, where the huge Puerto Rican flag flies, on the summit of what is now called Monte Carmelo.

Former Navy lands to the east of Monte Carmello now administered by the US Department of Fish and Wildlife

Tomás on Reportera

Horses

Many visitors and even some guidebooks talk about the wild horses of Vieques. In fact, these horses are not wild. They all have owners. Well, sort of.

The way it was explained to me was that if a horse upsets your garden or damages your car, that horse may very well not have an owner. On the other hand, if instead you were to take that same horse home, you can bet that its rightful owners would show up at your door demanding that you give them back their horse.

A Horse Story

A longtime resident of Vieques told me an interesting anecdote about horses and their owners.

Once upon a time, when the Marines were in Vieques, they decided that the horses grazing the fields inside the Camp Garcia gate were trespassing on government land.

The horses were rounded up, arrested, so to speak, and then put in a corral to be used for the horseback riding pleasure of the Marine brass.

One day, during a visit by the British Marines to Camp Garcia, a British Sergeant Major, passing by the corral, asked an American Sergeant Major about the horses in the camp. It was soon discovered that they both loved riding and the American Sergeant Major invited the British Sergeant Major out for a ride.

Late that afternoon the two Sergeant Majors saddled up two of the finest horses in the camp and rode out towards Esperanza. When they passed the Don Q Bar on the way into town, the two Sergeant Majors developed a keen thirst and decided to go into the bar for a few drinks.

The two officers tied up the horses to a tree and walked into the bar where they sat down and very knowledgeably discussed horses, horsemanship and their favorite places to ride.

The American Sergeant Major described to the British Sergeant Major every detail of the trail that the two men would take as soon as they had satiated their thirst. This being accomplished, they got off of their barstools and walked out onto the street.

When the two Sergeant Majors looked over at the tree where they had left the horses tied, they saw a pair of fancy saddles, a pair of bridles, and a pair of saddle blankets, in effect, all their riding paraphernalia, but there were no horses. The owner of the horses had recognized them and had taken them back.

There was too much gear to walk back to the camp. So they sat down at the bar, tossed down a series of stiff drinks and waited for transportation to take them and their equipment back to the base.

Carlos Conde on Diosa

Paso Fino

Juan Ponce de Leon brought the first horses to the New World from Spain in 1509. The horses were used for conquest and colonization. Ponce de Leon took 50 horses from Puerto Rico on his search for the fountain of youth. Francisco Pizarro used horses that he bought in Puerto Rico for the conquest in South America. Gasper Troche imported horses from Puerto Rico selling them in Mexico. After a brief flirtation with gold mining, horses became the most important export in Puerto Rico.

The horses that were brought to Puerto Rico were a blend of Berber and Spanish breeds. Later they were mixed with other pure breeds to produce a horse well adapted to the conditions in Puerto Rico. In short, the Paso Fino is the result of 500 years of selective breeding.

In addition to their uses by the military, Paso Finos were a primary means of transportation and were also employed for working cattle. Today they are used for shows, competitions and trail riding.

The Paso Fino is noted for its lateral gait and its smooth ride. The rider does not bounce up and down like on most horses; the Paso Fino's back stays level, three hooves on the ground and one in the air. The gait is instinctual, not trained. The footfall of the Paso Fino is right hind, right front, left hind, left front in a perfect four beat gait with uniform timing (isochronal) and equal strides (isometric), the hooves making the classic sound *taca taca taca taca*.

Paso Finos are beautiful, powerful horses. They have long full forelocks and manes and their tails flow almost to the ground ending in a tuft. Their hooves are extremely tough so that it is usually not necessary to shoe them.

On Vieques as well as in Puerto Rico, Colombia, Venezuela and the United States, Paso Finos are entered into exciting competitions where they are judged for Bella Forma (Good Form), Elegance and Comfort, Good Size and Solid Color, and Andadura (speed without breaking the pure four beat - *taca taca taca taca* gait).

Paso Finos can be very valuable. It is told that in the 1930s, President Trujillo of the Dominican Republic sent a blank check to Señor Genaro Cautiño to buy the famous Paso Fino horse called Dulce Sueño. The check was returned. Dulce Sueño was not for sale.

Playa Cofí

Playa Cofí is a sandy beach located less than a mile west of the heart of Isabel Segunda. To get there, turn north (or right, if coming from Isabel Segunda) on the road just east of the Kike Car Wash. Continue as far as you dare once the road turns to dirt.

The beach lies at the bottom of an approximately twenty-foot-high cliff, but can be accessed by a natural foot path over a rocky outcropping. The descent to the beach is not particularly difficult, but it is not recommended for those in poor physical condition or lack confidence in their basic rock scrambling abilities.

Playa Cofí got its name from the Puerto Rican pirate Roberto Cofresí, who plied the waters of Vieques and Puerto Rico in the early part of the nineteenth century. There are all sorts of stories surrounding the exploits of Cofresí and his pirate crew. Some legends claim he was a murdering cutthroat, others claim he was a Robin Hood type, stealing from the rich and giving to the poor.

There is talk of buried treasure left by Cofresí in Rincón in western Puerto Rico and also on Vieques in Tamarindo del Sur, in Martinez and in caves on Mount Pirata.

"There it exists - and the fishermen have seen it- boxes tied with chains and chains tied to the trunks of trees." (J. Pastor Ruiz)

At any rate, history tells us that in 1824, Cofresí and his buccaneers attacked and plundered as many as eight vessels. One of these plundered ships was flying the United States flag, and this time Cofresí's attack led to the deployment of the Schooner, USS Grampus, under the command of a Captain John Sloat.

The Captain's orders were to find and capture the notorious pirate. Cofresí and his crew put up a good fight, but in the end they were defeated and Cofresí was taken prisoner.

In March of 1825, Roberto Cofresí, who was turned over to Spanish authorities, was executed by firing squad in San Juan at the El Morro Fortress.

Egrets

Walking east along the sand, you will come to a small lagoon formed by the Quebrada Cofí. At sunset, hundreds of snowy egrets come to roost in a tree on the east side of the quebrada, such that, if one doesn't look too closely, it seems that the tree is dripping with large white fruits.

Sea Glass

Sea glass collectors will be amazed at the vast quantity of these broken pieces of colored glass that have been washed and polished by the action of the waves for years. The glass comes from a landfill that existed many years ago on the next beach to the east of Playa Cofí called Playa Muerta. (Presently known as Sea Glass Beach)

The prevailing winds, waves and currents have brought, and continue to bring, the sea glass to Playa Cofí.

La Lanchita

Located in Bravos de Boston, La Lanchita is a fine swimming beach.

During the winter, storms in the Atlantic create large swells that eventually come ashore on the north side of the island as breaking waves. When this happens, the north facing La Lanchita beach becomes a popular destination for surfers and boogie boarders.

El Oeste - The West

Western Vieques (Former NAF)

Western Vieques is the most fertile area of the island. The terrain is diversified. There are grass covered rolling hills, dry forests, mangrove lagoons, coconut groves, wetlands, magnificent beaches and the steep mountain slopes of Monte Pirata, the highest mountain on Vieques.

> The road to Punta Arenas runs almost parallel to the sea and between the road and the ocean are parcels of land where Viequense families have planted mango, citrus, sugar apple and gooseberry trees as well as all the varieties of commonly found flowers.
>
> In Martínez there is an old cemetery.
>
> The road continues toward Punta Arenas, which is the westernmost part of the island. Here, there is a dock where in better times a launch owned by the Benítez family made the crossing to Ceiba in one hour. Today all this is restricted, from Peña to Punta Arenas; the Navy has taken all these lands, which were in fact the most fertile on Vieques. The landowners were expropriated and their little houses demolished.
>
> Today you might find the remnants of old foundations or pieces of abandoned pipes and alongside a site where you can see that there once was a house, you might find a little mango or lime tree or an abandoned rosebush that a loving hand planted for the delight and solace of the family."

From *Vieques Antiguo y Moderno* by J. Pastor Ruiz, 1947

In colonial times this area was dedicated in most part to sugarcane production, with large sugar plantations dominating the land and its inhabitants. In the 1940s, the US Navy expropriated this land and used it for a munitions storage area, which they called the Naval Ammunition Facility (NAF).

Photo Courtesy of the US Department of Fish & Wildlife

Disposition of the Western Lands

On January 31, 2000, President William Clinton issued an executive directive instructing the Navy to return all 8,000 acres in the former Naval Ammunition Facility to the government of Puerto Rico.

Congress changed the directive and the result was that only 4,000 acres were returned to the Municipality of Vieques, 3,100 acres (the former Navy Conservation Zone) were transferred to the Department of the Interior, 700 acres to the Puerto Rico Department of Natural Resources and 200 acres (the ROTHR site and the radar installation at the top of Mount Pirata) were kept by the Navy.

Photo Courtesy of the US Department of Fish & Wildlife

Airport

The first airport in Vieques was nothing more than a 2,000-foot dirt runway, the remains of which are next to the highway east of the pier. The airstrip was constructed in the 1940s and paved in 1961. It was used primarily by the Navy and a few private planes from San Juan and St. Croix.

The first commercial plane to land there was a Carib Air flight that came specifically to pick up a woman who was seriously ill. The woman taken to the hospital in San Juan was the mother of the founder of Vieques' home airline, Osvaldo Gonzalez.

A long struggle ensued over the air rights to and from Vieques with the Navy allowing only a limited corridor of passage for essential marine and air transportation for residents. No commercial flights were allowed, thus severely limiting Vieques' ability to develop a tourist industry.

The old airstrip was eventually replaced by the Antonio Rivera Rodriquez Airport with a 3,400-foot runway.

On February 28, 2000, 110 acres of land were transferred to the Municipality of Vieques allowing for the expansion of the runway to 4,300 feet. The airport can now accommodate the 42 passenger ATR Turbo Prop Aircraft used by American Eagle.

Osvaldo Gonzalez

As a young boy, Osvaldo Gonzalez, more commonly known as Val, was fascinated by the Navy planes on maneuvers, which often performed air acrobatics, pirouettes and loop de loops.

Val moved to Chicago in the 1940s because of lack of opportunity in Vieques. He was drafted into the army by mistake when he was 17 years old. Another young man with the same name had not shown up and Val was drafted in his place. When the mistake was uncovered, Val insisted on staying in the army.

Later Val learned to fly at Ravenswood Airport before it became O'Hare and got a job with Midway airlines. He went back to Vieques and worked as a pilot for Bohlke International out of St. Croix.

In 1964, Val started Vieques Air Link (VAL) with a single leased aircraft. He borrowed $1,200 and made a down payment on his first plane, a three-passenger Cessna 162.

It was a one man show, with Osvaldo Gonzalez serving as pilot, ticket agent, mechanic and baggage handler.

The fare to Humacao was $4.00 and to San Juan $7.00.

In 1989, all of Vieques Airlink's aircraft were destroyed in Hurricane Hugo, but like the Phoenix rising from the ashes, Vieques Air Link regained its position as the leading airline in Vieques.

Photo by Kim Chan

W Hotel Resort & Spa

In its sixth annual list of "IT" hotels around the globe, *Travel + Leisure* chose Starwood's signature W Resort & Spa on Vieques as one of the world's best new hotels. It is the only full scale international brand hotel on the island, where accommodations consist mainly of small, quaint inns and bed and breakfasts.

Photo by Kim Chan

The Old Ceiba Tree

Just west of the airport on Route 200, there is a huge Ceiba tree, which is said to be more than 300 years old. As far back as anyone remembers, this ancient tree has served as a landmark site, where families and friends would often gather. Before the construction of the new airport, pilots seeking to land on Vieques used the tree to mark the far end of the dirt runway.

In this photo Paulina Conde stands at the base of the Ceiba with her mother and four sisters.

Left to Right: Liduvina "Lulu" Felix, Corporina Fragoza, Ursula Felix, Juana "Juanita" Encarnación de Felix (Mami), Carmen Gladys Felix, Paulina Felix de Conde

La Peña

The beach that lies parallel to the road between Punta Caballo (near the airport) and the Rompeolas (Mosquito Pier) is called La Peña.

Running behind the beach is a dirt road, which has a small bridge at the point where the road crosses a narrow quebrada. Legend has it, that if you should see an elegantly dressed woman pushing a baby carriage over the bridge at night, do not stop to converse with her. If you ask to see the baby, she will push aside the hood of the carriage and you will find yourself staring at the devil and he will steal your soul.

Devils notwithstanding, this is a beautiful beach, easy to get to and you'll be just about guaranteed to have the whole beach to yourself, weekend or not, high season or low.

Mosquito Pier

The Mosquito Pier is a mile-long seawall, which is often referred to as the *Rompeolas,* meaning "breakwater." Once onsite, you will easily understand the concept. Looking to the east, you'll feel the wind in your face and see waves breaking against the seawall. If you turn the other way, you'll see tranquil turquoise waters with barely a ripple of waves.

The reason being is that Vieques lies in the zone of the trade winds. These winds are usually consistent, blowing east to west. Consequently, the waves arrive from more or less the same direction and break on the eastern side of the Rompeolas leaving the western or leeward side almost perfectly calm.

United States Takeover

In the 1880s, United States foreign policy was heavily influenced by Alfred T. Mahan who served as a strategist and consultant to the US Government. Mahan proposed a shift in military strategy from an emphasis on ground warfare to naval power.

To ensure this naval superiority, he felt that the United States should establish a "Great White Fleet" of armor-plated, steam-powered battleships. He proposed the takeover of Hawaii, the Philippines and strategically located islands in the Caribbean with the establishment of US naval bases in these locations. Moreover, he advocated the construction of a canal between the Caribbean Sea and the Pacific Ocean so the US warships could move more easily between the two oceans.

Spanish American War

On February 15, 1898 the battleship *Maine* was blown up while at anchor in Havana Harbor. Some three hundred United States Marines lost their lives in the explosion.

Although neither the cause nor the perpetrators of the incident were ever discovered, the US press, in a series of sensational articles that appeared in newspapers across the nation, laid the blame on "cowardly Spanish operatives" who had placed mines on the battleship's hull, detonating them from the shore.

The American public was outraged and shortly after the *Maine* incident, the United States declared war against Spain. The Spanish American War was of short duration and resulted in a complete victory for the United States.

In the treaty that followed the Spanish surrender, Spain turned Guam and the Philippines over to the United States and renounced all claims to her remaining Caribbean colonies. Cuba was granted independence, except in matters of foreign policy and Puerto Rico was turned over outright to the United States.

(1898 was also the year that the United States, in an action that had nothing to do with the Spanish American War, annexed the Hawaiian Islands.)

Building the Great Seawall

In the late 1930s, the threat of war in Europe loomed over the United States of America. Military interests focused on Puerto Rico as a mainstay in the defense of the Caribbean and especially of the Panama Canal.

The plan was to construct a seawall that would extend from Vieques to the Roosevelt Roads Naval Base in Ceiba on the Big Island and to create a naval facility in the Atlantic surpassing even the Pearl Harbor Naval Base in Hawaii.

The base was to be fully equipped and large enough to contain most of the US Atlantic Fleet as well as the entire British Fleet, if and when Great Britain fell to the Germans.

When the Navy arrived to begin this massive project, Vieques was in serious trouble economically. The decline of the sugar industry in conjunction with food shortages caused by the war created a condition of massive poverty and rampant unemployment. Thus, despite the social, economic and emotional devastation of the expropriation and the forced relocation of the people living on these lands, the promise of employment on the Navy project left the Viequenses with some hope.

In fact, the Navy hired 1,700 Viequenses along with 1,000 laborers from the Big Island to build the giant sea wall and to construct concrete weapons storage warehouses called magazines, which were to be cut into the hills of western Vieques and camouflaged by a covering of grasslands.

The workers were paid $2.25 per day. Laborers, working three shifts a day, dug out a mountain and used the dirt and rocks to fill in the sea.

"They worked 24 hours a day. There was no rest. There were no objections to allowing this flow of North American money. This money, for the most part was collected by contractors from the United States and San Juan. Employees came every week from different sections of Puerto Rico. Nonetheless, much of the profits remained in Vieques.

"For two years the town swam in gold. Rents went up three to four times that which was normally paid. People bought fine clothing and treated it without due consideration. Alcoholic beverages were consumed without measure.

"There were those who would wash their floors with beer and those who would buy a $35 dollar suit on Saturday and wear it on Monday to mix concrete and it would be ruined after two hours. 'The Base is here, and it will bring more,' they would say."
(Translated from *Vieques Antiguo y Moderno* by J. Pastor Ruiz)

The project was stopped in midstream due to two historical events. The German Army had become bogged down in Russia and the tide of the war appeared to have changed in favor of the Allies, while the attack on Pearl Harbor challenged the military wisdom of concentrating an entire fleet in one area.

In 1943, the construction of the pier, which was at that time about one mile long, was discontinued. The Viequenses were left worse off than ever. With the massive land expropriations, there was no chance for employment in the sugar industry. Furthermore, the ability of the people to at least continue subsistence activities such as having small gardens, raising animals, hunting crabs, fishing, charcoal making and the gathering of coconuts and wild fruits was also severely curtailed.

"This boom of ready cash never compensated for many of the setbacks caused by the naval base. The richest and most fertile lands were expropriated by the Navy. The neighborhoods of Tapón, Mosquito and La Llave all disappeared. All the neighbors and small landowners left to the new neighborhoods of Moscú and Montesanto. Families that had their little house, cows, a horse and some farmland went on to have nothing more than a makeshift shack, a fistful of coins and the night and the day.

"Those that had a garden plot and who lived happily as tenants surrounded by farmlands and fruit trees now live crowded together lacking even air with which to breathe."
Translated from *Vieques Antiguo y Moderno* by J. Pastor Ruiz, 1947

In 2000, the Mosquito Pier was included in the 4,000 acre transfer of land from the US Navy to the Municipality of Vieques.

Today, the one-mile-long pier is used recreationally as a place to picnic, fish or to simply relax and enjoy the ocean breezes one mile away from shore. In the late afternoon it is a favorite destination for walkers, joggers and bicyclists. As of this writing, the future of the pier is in limbo, but there is talk of using it for the ferry and cargo terminals, which would provide for a shorter route to Ceiba on the Big Island.

Victoria The Manta Ray - From our Travel Journal, June 23, 2003:

...after dinner we made our way to the pier. There were just three fishermen, sitting there at the time. We walked over to the edge of the pier and within minutes this manta ray cruised right by us. It swam just below the surface and close up against the dock. It was a big, beautiful manta ray, black with white spots on its wings. It swam slowly just a few feet from the edge of the pier starting from where the lights began and continuing until it reached an area of darkness. Then it would make a wide circle, go around and come back to the beginning of the lights.

The big manta ray illuminated by the dock lights and cruising so close to us on that quiet starry tropical night had a surreal quality that served almost to hypnotize those of us observing from above.

It seems everyone was talking about this manta ray that people called Victoria. So a few nights later, we returned to the pier to see Victoria again. We arrived a bit earlier that night, around ten o'clock, and there were about a hundred people there. Cars were lined up on both sides of the pier. People were hanging over the dock and along the railing above.

People were selling stuff out of trucks set up with beach umbrellas. A man and a woman were baking clams on a grill and offering them for sale. Another couple was selling pinchos (skewers of barbecued meat).

Some people had brought chairs and were stretched out relaxing, but there was no manta ray. There were calamari. There were big silvery tarpon. But no manta ray. A man with a video camera and other sophisticated photographic equipment told us that Victoria had not shown up yet and that he heard that she wasn't there the night before or the night before that. Maybe she would show up later that night, or maybe Victoria was just taking a break.

Meanwhile, people didn't seem to care. It was a party, everyone just watching out for that manta ray.

We don't know if Victoria came back that night or not, but we left and figured we'd return when it wasn't a weekend or maybe later at night, just in case Victoria was shy with so many people hanging around.

We came back to the pier a few nights later. There were people and food vendors and there was Victoria, replete with an entourage of remoras swimming just above and just below her. And she was putting on quite a show. When she got by the center of the crowd, she'd rise to the surface and the people would cheer. Then when she reached the end of the lights, she would bank like a jet plane when it makes a turn putting one white-spotted wing into the air and then she'd swim around for another pass and more applause.

The people were thrilled. Men and women, little children and teenagers, tourists and locals, all enthralled by the spectacular Manta Ray Show. It seemed to us that eco-tourism is alive and well on the island of Vieques.

Photo by Ura Connelly

Mosquito Beach

There is a small beach just west of the Mosquito Pier (*Las Rompeolas*), which is a popular venue for weekend parties, picnics and barbecues.

This is also a good place to get in the water and snorkel the calm waters on this leeward side of the Rompeolas. Here you will have the opportunity to see an interesting variety of sea creatures that have made their homes in the rocks that support the mile-long pier.

To get to the beach, drive onto the Mosquito Pier and make the first left turn onto a dirt track. Follow the dirt road to the beach.

Expropriation

To obtain land for the proposed Naval base in Vieques, the United States government initiated a series of expropriations in which the privately held lands on Vieques would be turned over to the Navy.

The expropriation and the dislocation of thousands of people were relatively easy for the Navy because of the concentration of the lands in the hands of a few large estate owners. For example, one single owner in the *Barrio* of Punta Arenas owned some 3,000 acres of land on which were 62 houses.

Although some of the families had been living in these homes for generations, they held no title to their property, but had rather made informal agreements with the landowners.

When the land was expropriated, the families living there lost not only their homes, gardens, animals and any other possessions they could not immediately take with them, but they lost their jobs as well. This all occurred in a time period of between 24 hours and ten days, depending on the case.

Most people received no advance warning at all. They were simply informed by the estate owner that they had to leave their homes immediately. Those fortunate enough to get a ten day notice received the following eviction document written in English:

> The house and land which you occupy in the Municipality of Vieques was acquired by the United States under judgment of the Federal Court which granted the right of immediate possession. You will be required to vacate this property within ten days from the start of this notice. Should you wish to move to another site on Federal property you will be assigned to a suitable area by the Officer-in-Charge of the Project upon execution by you of an agreement setting forth the terms upon which your occupancy of the site is permitted.
> *Signed by J. C. Gebhard, Captain (CEC) U.S.N..*

Almost three quarters of the island ended up in Navy hands. The displaced families were relocated into the center of the island onto razed sugar cane fields marked off in 200-square-foot plots. They were not given title to this land, not allowed to exchange lots and were told that they could face eviction with a notice of 24 hours at the Navy's discretion.

Cruz Cordero Ventura in her book *Vieques, Sesenta Años de Bombardeos en Tiempos de Paz*, (Vieques, Sixty Years of Bombing in Times of Peace) remembers:

"They gave us a paper that said we had to leave within 24 hours. My parents had two wooden houses. We had animals such as chickens, pigs, goats, horses and cows. For us, this was everything. The horse was our means of transportation; to go shopping, to go to the doctor.

"In spite of being very poor, we lived well. We grew everything on our land, all kinds of fruits and vegetables which we shared with everyone.

"My father was a hard worker and he maintained four gardens in which were planted bananas, plantains, potatoes, yautía, oranges and all kinds of vegetables. He even learned how to grow rice and how to prepare it. In the house where we lived, we had 20 mango trees, which people called the mango grove of Don Domingo, which was my father's name.

"As I was only 11 years old, I did not understand my father's great anguish. The worst was that we could not sell anything that we had because everyone else was in the same position. We had to go and leave everything: animals, crops and our dreams. Nobody cared and nobody helped us....

"It is still fresh in my mind the moment that my father with the aid of my brothers put all of our belongings onto a rented truck. We had to make the move in one trip for that was all my father could afford.

We loaded as much as we could with the help of the driver. As there were so few trucks in those days, they gave preference to those who had to take apart their house, and being that ours was just a move, we had to do it in the middle of the night.

"Everybody was in a state of panic, taking down their houses before the bulldozer came and left us with nothing, because they had threatened that if we did not leave on time, they would tear down the house, with everything in it, whether there were people inside or not.

"I remember the neighbors commenting that you have to get up early to gather everything before the 'pig' arrives. That is what the people called the bulldozer."
(Translated from the original Spanish.)

La Capilla Ecuménica (Ecumenical Chapel)

On April 19, 1999, Viequense security guard, David Sanes, was killed by a 500-pound bomb that missed its target and exploded near the observation post where he was working. The incident led to a civil disobedience protest characterized by the establishment of occupied camps within the bombing range, thus preventing further bombing. The people living in of one of these camps built a chapel on the beach called Playa Icacos.

The chapel became the spiritual center of the movement. Priests gave mass there, holy water was sprinkled on bomb craters and unexploded ordnance in the target zone. The Archbishop of San Juan, Roberto González gave a sermon at the chapel about civil disobedience. The Bishop of Caguas, Puerto Rico, Monsignor Alvaro Corrada del Rio, brought a statue of the Virgin del Carmen, the patron saint of fishermen and blessed it.

The chapel was damaged by Hurricane Lenny, but was rebuilt as soon as the storm had passed.

On May 4, 2000, the day when all those present at the camps were arrested and removed from the bombing range, the chapel was occupied by nuns and religious leaders who were inside praying. Heavily armed agents of the Navy, the FBI, Federal Marshals and the Puerto Rico Police Department, many wearing bulletproof vests and helmets with plastic shields or gas masks, stormed the church. They handcuffed the priests and nuns and threw them into military vehicles. Navy bulldozers demolished the chapel, but somehow the chapel bell was preserved.

In 2002, with the support of the government in Puerto Rico, a replica of the chapel was constructed on the hillside directly across the street from the Capitol Building in San Juan. The original church bell was recovered and placed in the new chapel.

The chapel became the scene of confrontations between pro-Navy supporters and those who wanted the Navy to leave Vieques as well as between statehood advocates and separatists.

In 2003, the governor of Puerto Rico decided to send the chapel back to Vieques where it was to be relocated across the road from the Camp Garcia gate and serve as part of the transfer ceremonies on the first of May, when the Navy was to leave Vieques.

Unfortunately, Big Island officials did not include Viequenses in the church relocation plan, which resulted in logistical complications. The Ecumenical Chapel arrived at Isabel Segunda on a barge leased by the Puerto Rican government.

Meanwhile, as anyone who has spent time in Vieques could tell you, it is impossible to move something as wide as the chapel through the narrow streets of the town. This problem soon became apparent to those in charge of the relocation, who now realized that the chapel would have to leave Isabel Segunda by sea and be offloaded somewhere else on the island. (A better alternative might have been offloading the chapel at Playa Caracas and transporting it through the camp.)

But it was too late. The government leased barge was long gone.

Many times things on Caribbean islands move at a slower pace than they do

elsewhere. A slower pace can also be expected for government related activities, not only in the Caribbean, but just about anywhere in the world. Such was the case with the chapel relocation.

A second barge was eventually sent from the Big Island to Vieques. The barge turned out to be too small to safely carry the chapel, so back it went to the Big Island.

By the time a third and more suitable barge arrived in Vieques, the transfer ceremonies were well underway and it was too late to follow the original plan of locating the chapel across from the camp gate.

Alternatively, the Ecumenical Chapel was taken to the Rompeolas, offloaded, and trucked to the former Navy occupied lands on western Vieques. Here it stands today, overlooking the beautiful Vieques Sound, a symbol of peace where preparations for war were once the order of the day.

Laguna Kiani

At the Laguna Kiani you will have an excellent opportunity to observe a beautiful mangrove lagoon from the comfort of a wooden boardwalk constructed through the mangroves and ending in two viewing decks.

Parking is available at the entrance to the boardwalk where there is also an informative display of photos, illustrations and written information about the mangrove environment and its importance to the tropical ecology.

Oscar Díaz, former head of the US Department of Fish and Wildlife, reported that the Kiani Lagoon is also bioluminescent. This area is closed to the public during the night so you will not be able to observe this phenomenon.

Fishing and swimming are also not permitted because of contamination caused by the dumping of toxic wastes in the lagoon during the years of the Navy occupation.

Magazines

The Navy used the western lands principally for weapons and ammunition storage, which they called the Naval Ammunition Facility, or NAF.

The armaments were stored in large concrete warehouses called magazines that were cut into the hills of western Vieques and then covered with earth and planted in grass.

The older WWII magazines were smaller and considerably more camouflaged than those built later on. This was because the warplanes used in World War II flew at slower speeds and at lower altitudes than those built after the war. The shift in the degree of camouflage came about because the crews of the slower and lower flying aircraft would have a better chance to see what was happening on the land than later faster and higher flying planes.

Playa Grande

The remains of the once rich Playa Grande Sugar Central lie within the bush just to the west of the ROTHR facility. There is a rough trail leading from the road to the sprawling ruins.

Playa Grande was the largest sugar operation, or *central*, in Vieques. It had been operating from the mid 19th century, when it was one of eight *centrales*, until its expropriation by the US Navy in 1941.

Agriculture, principally the cultivation and processing of sugar cane, was the mainstay of the Vieques economy,

"In 1920, three of the five *centrales* produced 17,276 tons of sugar. Moreover, Vieques produced enormous quantities of milk, meats, fruits and vegetables. So important was the industry that workers from neighboring islands including Puerto Rico flocked to Vieques in search of work."
Vieques Antiguo y Moderno, J. Pastor Ruiz

The Playa Grande Central as well as the Esperanza Central, used trains to move the sugar cane from the plantation fields to the factory for processing and on the piers at Mosquito and Punta Arenas for export.

Besides the Playa Grande ruins a few other remnants of the once thriving sugar industry are still in existence.

The remains of the dock where sugar and molasses were once loaded onto ships for exportation as well as the large iron tanks once used to store molasses still can be seen at the beach in Punta Arenas.

Across from the Green Store in Esperanza, you can find the ruins of the Esperanza Central's old mechanical workshop and the locomotive once used to haul railroad cars loaded with stalks of sugar cane and barrels of sugar and molasses.

Ruins of the Esperanza Central's mechanical workshop

The Sugar Industry in Vieques

Spain did not consolidate its control over Vieques until the middle of the 19th century. When Vieques did become stable enough for a plantation economy, it attracted well-to-do inhabitants of other Caribbean islands, notably the French colonies of Martinique and Guadeloupe. Discouraged by slave rebellions at home, they sold their holdings and established plantations on Vieques.

Five large sugar estates, or *centrales*, Arcadia, Esperanza, Playa Grande, Santa Elena and Santa María owned almost all the farmable lands on the island. Enslaved workers provided the labor for the first sugar plantations. By the latter part of the century, however, most European nations had abolished slavery. (In Puerto Rico, slavery ended in 1873.)

On Vieques, planters reacted to this turn of events by utilizing local laborers known as *agregados*, who would live on the plantations and imported laborers called *jornaleros*. Employment was sporadic and wages were low.

The majority of sugar cane laborers on Vieques were *jornaleros*. These workers lived in barracks and moved from *central* to *central* when and if jobs were available. When there was no work, they had to rely on odd jobs or do without.

The lot of the *agregados* was somewhat better. They were given small plots of land on the plantation. They did not have title to the land and lived there at the whim of the owners. Although this situation encouraged exploitation, at least the *agregados* had the opportunity to provide for themselves when they wasn't any work. They could plant subsistence crops in their *conucos*, or little gardens and they had access to the plantation lands on the coast where they could fish, gather coconuts, pick *caracoles* (whelks) or dive for conch and lobster. They could also hunt *jueyes* (land crabs) in the flats and collect wood for charcoal in the forests.

Laborers from the English colonies, many of whom were ex slaves, arrived from Nevis, St. Kitts, Anguilla, Antigua, Tortola, Virgin Gorda and Jost Van Dyke, and from the Danish colonies of St. Thomas, St. John and St. Croix. There were so many workers who had come from Tortola that *Tortoleño* was often used as a generic term to describe a black worker.

While the Spanish still remained in power, there were two major incidents in which workers rebelled against the unfair system under which they toiled. In 1864, workers from the English colonies at the Hacienda Resolución staged a protest demanding that one of their fellow workers who was arrested and jailed by the sugar plantation owner be released. The Spanish military intervened and several protesters were incarcerated at the fort.

Although these workers were legally free, the labor situation in Vieques was tantamount to slavery. In 1871, the Government of Vieques passed the *Reglamento Especial Para el Peonaje Extranjero*, or the Special Regulation Concerning Foreign Workers. Among other things, this law obliged foreign workers to live on the haciendas on which they worked and demanded complete obedience to the plantation owner and governmental authorities.

In 1874, hundreds of black workers at the Playa Grande Sugar Estate rebelled against their mistreatment by the plantation owners and the government. The Spanish Civil Guard intervened, killing one worker and wounding several others. The protest lasted several weeks. Men, women and children attacked the soldiers with sticks and stones and burned the sugar fields. Dozens were arrested and incarcerated at the fort.

Sugar cane work was low paid and sporadic. The harvest called the *zafra* lasted from March until June. This consisted of cutting cane and then loading it onto bull carts or railway cars, which would take the cane to the mill for processing or to be put on boats bound for the Big Island.

July and August were dedicated to fertilizing, planting, weeding and cleaning drainage ditches. September to February, while the cane was growing, was called the *invernazo*, or dead time. There was little to no work and even less money. The *agregados* survived as best they could by subsistence activities such as fishing, gardening and charcoal burning. The *jornaleros*, who lacked these opportunities, often were reduced to desperate straits.

In his book, *Vieques Antiguo y Moderno*, J. Pastor Ruiz describes the daily life of a sugar cane worker:

> The workday was from sunrise to sunset, at times 12-14 hours a day … the wages paid were 50 cents a day, whether for planting, digging, irrigation or weeding. The same for cutting the cane and carting it away in bull carts. All were paid the same.
>
> In Vieques, there was a special circumstance, which was the abundance of English workers. These English of color were very strong workers. They lived in barracks on the haciendas. These laborers were called *negradas*. Their specialty was gathering cane and making bundles of 40-50 cane stalks, which they tied together with a loose rope. Using a cloth over their heads, they would bend down, gather up the bundle and carry it to the carts that brought the cane to the mill. Sometimes they would work from 2:00 in the morning until 8:00 at night.

In 1898, Puerto Rico, along with Vieques and Culebra, were taken over by the United States. Many thought that under the new rulers the deplorable economic situation would change for the better. The North Americans, however, were primarily interested in the islands for strategic reasons and gave little to no consideration to the existing problems. Although the sugar industry boomed in the first decade of the 20th century and the population of the island increased, the plight of the average worker went from bad to worse.

Under United States rule, in 1915, workers organized a strike against the sugar barons demanding a raise in salary from 50 cents a day to $1.00 a day and a reduction of the workday from 14 hours to eight hours. The plantation owners called in the police who killed several strikers and wounded many others. Dozens were arrested and incarcerated at the fort.

During the Great Depression, the problems of poverty and unemployment were even worse on Vieques than on the Big Island. It was so bad that when the US Virgin Islands opened up immigration to citizens of Puerto Rico, thousands of Viequenses left for St. Croix, whose sugar industry, although failing, at least still existed.

A 1939 *El Mundo* headline read: "The Island of Vieques is being deserted: families migrate by the hundreds to St. Croix hoping to escape the horrible situation of misery there."

A report made by an agricultural team sent to Vieques by the Puerto Rican Government concluded that:

> …the tragedy of Vieques is analogous to that of Puerto Rico, only much more serious. Thirty three thousand acres of land are hoarded, for the most part by two large sugar corporations. Eleven thousand residents are living on what little remains of the land. A very rich island, with every kind of fruit, fish and livestock is impeded from developing its full agricultural and industrial potential. The per capita income scarcely reaches the ridiculous level of $22 per year."
> (Translated from *La Agonía Industrial de Vieques*, "Puerto Rico Ilustrado," 1937, by Tomás Jesus de Castro.)

The sugar industry on Vieques gasped its last breath in the 1940s with the expropriation of the lands formerly owned by the Playa Grande Estate. Today, it's difficult to even find a sugar cane plant on Vieques.

ROTHR

The Relocatable Over the Horizon Radar (ROTHR) facility on Vieques was originally installed to be used in the "War on Drugs" and to monitor the activities of leftist insurgents operating in Colombia and other countries of South America.

The radar station was to be placed in the western lands where the Navy had planted a grove of 1,300 mahogany trees in an effort to comply with the Memorandum of Understanding, an agreement in which the Navy, in exchange for the dropping of a multimillion-dollar lawsuit against them, had promised to make an effort to stimulate the local economy and mitigate the environmental damage caused by the use of the lands as a bombing range.

The radar facility would occupy 100 acres and include 34 transmitting towers with an average height of about 100 feet.

Vieques protesters picketed the public hearings on the ROTHR facility that took place at the Alcaldía. They expressed concerns about the health risks of electromagnetic radiation, the fact that the ROTHR complex would consume 50% of the electricity supply of the Municipality of Vieques and the military use of lands, which the citizens hoped would some day be used for ecologically sensitive development.

The ROTHR project served to unite the community. Groups that had never taken a stand before and even former staunch supporters of the Navy presence in Vieques joined in with anti-bombing protesters to express their vehement opposition to the radar installation.

Despite the controversy, the ROTHR was put into operation and remains on Navy-owned property. The 1,300 mahogany trees were cleared to make way for the construction.

Punta Arenas ("Green Beach")

Route 200 leads to the western coast of the island and Playa Punta Arenas. Renamed by the Navy, Green Beach, Punta Arenas is located on the northwestern corner of Vieques and has magnificent views of the Big Island just six miles away. The coconut palm groves behind the beach are lush and full.

Spend the day picnicking, swimming, snorkeling or just relaxing in a beach chair or on a hammock stretched between two palm trees.

The bad news is that the low lying, leeward location of the beach and the vast mangrove lagoons in the area create an environment favorable for a creature called the sand fly. These annoying little devils often come out in force in the early morning and late afternoon or when the wind is exceptionally still. A good strategy is to plan to leave the beach sometime before 4:00 P.M. and definitely before 6:00 P.M., when agents of the US Department of Fish and Wildlife close the gates leading back to the highway.

In days gone by, there was a dock on the beach, from where sugarcane and molasses were shipped to the Big Island for processing. Boats, often built in Vieques, went back and forth between Punta Arenas and the Big Island. Here one could find a ferry boat with a diesel engine, as well as several sloops, fishing boats and yolas powered by motor, sail and oar. Nearby was a store where people could buy just about anything they needed such as food, clothing, shoes, tools and cooking utensils.

All this changed with the Navy expropriations. People living in the area were forced to move to the center of the island. The dock and store were closed and the new route to the Big Island began in Isabel Segunda necessitating a two hour journey in less protected waters.

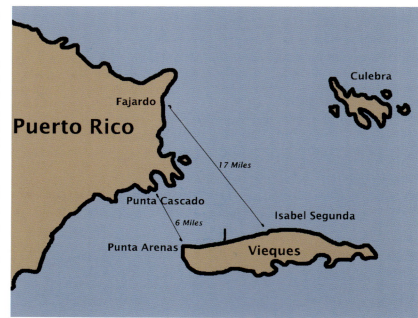

Punta Vaca

Southwestern Beaches

On the south coast of the former NAF are several beautiful, albeit challenging to get to, beaches.

Palmar

Playa Grande - A quebrada leading from the large Laguna Playa Grande empties into the sea at the center of the beach.

Playa Grande

El Sur - The South

Esperanza

Esperanza, the second largest town in Vieques, is located on the southern coast. It is a quaint fishing village that has become the center of tourism.

Along the main seaside street called the Malecón, you will find an array of bars, restaurants and guesthouses and a beautiful waterfront promenade.

Esperanza has a swimming beach, a boat launch and two docks, one of which belongs to the Fishermen's Association.

For those who prefer a larger beach with more facilities, the *balneario* or public beach at Sun Bay is just a short distance from Esperanza.

Photo by Christine Aliberti

La Tienda Verde, The Green Store

Photo by Christine Aliberti

Intimate Inns and quaint bed & breakfasts are the backbone of the Vieques accommodations industry.

Photo by Christine Aliberti

The Vieques Conservation and Historical Trust

The Vieques Conservation and Historical Trust, established in 1984, is a privately funded organization whose mission is to preserve the history and environment of Vieques and especially, the Bioluminescent Bay.

Visitors and locals alike have the unique opportunity to take advantage of the Trust's many facilities.

There is a resource room that contains a library, offers internet access, classes, films and Bioluminescent Bay information. Across the hall, the pre-Columbian room features artifacts and information about the life and customs of the indigenous peoples of Vieques and the Caribbean. A bookstore in the hall features books about Vieques and related topics, locally produced crafts and other items that can be purchased in the adjacent gift shop. The proceeds of all sales go to maintain the Trust. In the courtyard, behind the main building, is a marine life exhibit, which now include a room focusing on bioluminescence. An exhibit room and scientific laboratory can be found in the rear building. The exhibit room contains changing exhibits concerning the environment and history of Vieques.

University professors and students can make use of the scientific laboratory to carry out research on the bioluminescent bays.

Additionally, The Trust has launched a scholarship program funding 15 Viequense students and the MANTA Summer & Saturday Programs for children six to eleven years old interested in the natural environment and the sciences.

Ángel Rodríguez Cristóbal

A bust of Ángel Rodríguez Cristóbal stands overlooking the dock and the waterfront of the town of Esperanza, the inscription written by Juan Antonio Corretjer reads:

> The Fishermen's Association of Vieques, Inc. honors the memory of: Ángel Rodríguez Cristóbal 1946 - 1979
>
> When the cause is just, there is no need to fear."

Ángel Rodríguez Cristóbal was born April 2, 1946 in Ciales, Puerto Rico. At the age of 18, he entered into the United States Army. It was during his three year tour of active duty on the battlefield that he understood the injustices being committed against the people of Vietnam.

Upon his return to Puerto Rico, he became involved in agriculture in the town of Pozas de Ciales. He participated in the social and political movements of his town. In 1972, he joined the Puerto Rican Independent Party. Later, in 1974, he joined the Puerto Rican Socialist League. His militancy brought him, in the year 1978, to join the Viequense fishermen in their fight against the presence of the United States Navy in Vieques.

He was arrested on May 19, 1979, along with twenty other protesters from a group of 200 people who were participating in an act of religious civil disobedience on a beach in an area occupied by the Navy.

A federal judge, a lackey of the Navy, sentenced him to serve six months in a prison in Tallahassee, Florida. On November 11, 1979, he was murdered in his prison cell.

Hero and martyr, tireless fighter for his homeland.

…Upon his assassination, he enters the pantheon of the immortals whose deaths define a piece of Puerto Rican history.

(Translated from the original Spanish.)

Esperanza Beach

Sun Bay

Sun Bay is formed by Cayo de Tierra on the west and Punta Negra on the east, which reach outward to the south. These two points of land protect the bay from the full force of the easterly trade winds and Caribbean waves.

The beach at Sun Bay is a mile-long stretch of soft coral sand that extends into the bay, perfect for sunbathing and wading in the shallow water.

The idyllic tropical setting of Sun Bay was very likely influential in it being chosen as the location of the final scene of the 1960 movie, *Lord of the Flies*.

Sun Bay is fringed by tropical vegetation, most notably by the icon of the tropics, the coconut palm. At Sun Bay you will find two types of these palms, the tall native variety and the shorter, but fuller and bushier, dwarf coconut palm.

Other prominent shoreline vegetation includes sea grapes, beach mahos, almonds, and genips.

The View

Looking out from the beach you can enjoy a magnificent view of the turquoise-colored Caribbean waters, Punta Negra in the east, Mount Pirata, the highest mountain on the island, in the distance and two offshore cays, Cayo Afuera and Cayo de Tierra in the west.

Because the two cays look like humpback whales, they are sometimes referred to as *Las Ballenas*, the whales.

Balneario Sun Bay lies on the south coast of Vieques, just east of Esperanza.

The beach can be accessed near the southern end of Highway 997.

Sun Bay is owned by Puerto Rico National Parks and is the only beach on Vieques with public facilities. There is a two dollar per vehicle fee for parking.

Facilities include bathrooms, outdoor showers, public telephones, water fountains and garbage cans.

Convenient wooden benches are strategically placed in shady areas on the perimeter of the beach, which has bathing areas marked off by line and buoys.

Punta Negra

Swimming and Snorkeling

The water on the eastern corner of the beach tends to be calm and makes for enjoyable, relaxed swimming.

Snorkelers may be treated to the sighting of large starfish that often graze the patches of sea grass just offshore.

On windy days, the western end of the beach can be wavy enough to play in the surf.

Camping

Sun Bay has a camping area with barbecue facilities. (Call 787 741-8198 for campground information.)

Hiking

The dirt tracks that extend eastward from Sun Bay offer some fine hiking to destinations such as the Bio Bay, the salt pond behind Sun Bay, the dramatic Punta Negra Headland and a back road to Playa Media Luna.

Relaxing

Tie up a hammock between two coconut palms, bring a picnic lunch or a barbecue grill, lay back, relax, play on the beach and take a nice swim. Enjoy.

Mother's Day Battle At Sun Bay

On Mother's Day, May 11, 1997, Sun Bay was packed with local families. Then into this idyllic scene of picnicking, barbeques and kids swimming and playing on the beach, four warships from Holland and Belgium sailed into the bay and dropped anchor right off the public beach. The ships were there to participate in maneuvers along with the US Navy, a privilege for which they had paid a hefty sum of money.

The Viequenses were outraged. The situation with the Navy and the bombing was bad enough, but this had never happened before. Within minutes, a delegation of four fishing boats motored over to one of the ships. Using a bullhorn, one of the fishermen who spoke English, called to the commanders of the ships, beseeching them to leave the area.

In response, the Dutch sailors dispersed the small boats using high pressure fire hoses. The fishermen returned to the beach. They then enlisted other Viequenses and, armed with bottles of paint and rocks, a small flotilla of *yolas* returned to confront the mighty warships.

The fire hoses were again brought into play. Fortunately for the fishermen, however, the fire hoses could not be aimed directly downward, but rather outward and down.

The resulting arc provided a zone of protection for the Viequense fishermen, and the savvy captains immediately took advantage of the situation passing under the torrent and approached the ships.

Now with the fishing boats close to the hulls of the ships, the battle began in earnest.

The fishermen began to hurl bottles of paint defiling the clean shiny metal hulls of the warships. This tactic was employed because they had learned that the numbers on the ships were of great importance to someone in the Navy hierarchy who cared about such matters. If the numbers were somehow obscured, this would mean that the ship had to sail back to Roosevelt Roads, remove the splashed paint from the hull and repaint the numbers. This could take a day or more; a day when that ship would not be bombing Vieques.

In response to the Viequense attack, the sailors hurled beer cans, debris, tools and whatever else they could find at the fishermen. One protester, describing the scene, reported that he was struck in the head by a beer can, which, luckily for him was half empty. More ominously, seconds later, a heavy iron monkey wrench crashed into the cover of the outboard engine and cracked the cowling.

Undaunted by what was becoming a very dangerous situation, the fishermen continued their harassment of the battleships. After an almost two-hour confrontation in which a Dutch sailor lost an eye to a Viequense slingshot, the admiral of the fleet gave the order to haul anchor and leave the area. Just as in biblical times, David had once again defeated Goliath at least for this battle if not for the war.

Cayo de Tierra

Cayo de Tierra and Cayo Afuera lie off the coast of Esperanza between the town and Sun Bay. Cayo de Tierra is connected to the main island by a narrow sand spit and can be accessed by land.

Adventurers can hike to the top of the island where you can stand at the edge of the 100-foot cliffs with exciting views of the Caribbean, Sun Bay and much of the southern coast and low-lying interior of Vieques.

There are 127 identified species of birds on Vieques and Cayo de Tierra is an excellent venue for birdwatchers.

From the sand spit, you can often see three different varieties of terns: royal, sandwich and least. In the winter, look for white-cheeked pintail and blue-winged tealin the salt pond.

In the dry season, the water in the salt pond evaporates and you can scrape up natural sea salt containing all the minerals in the sea and all that are essential to the human body. On Vieques, this is the favored salt to use for ice cream churning.

To get to the top of the island, walk along the sand spit and then bear left following the coast on the east side of the island. The salt pond will be just inland to the west.

Keep walking until you reach the end of the salt pond, but before the beginning of the cliffs. Look for a trail through the sea grapes that leads to the salt pond. Once you get to the perimeter of the salt pond, follow one of the steep paths up to the top of the island.

Stand near the cliffs, feel the warm fragrant trade winds and from your lofty perch, observe the tropicbirds, pelicans and brown boobies sailing through the air below you.

Once up on top of the island, you can continue around the perimeter where you can scramble down the rocks and walk around the coast.

There is a beautiful beach just before you return to the sand spit from where you originally crossed over to the island. A refreshing swim here might be a welcome experience after your hike around the island.

Sandbar between Sun Bay and Cayo de Tierra

View of Esperanza Bay, Sun Bay and the salt pond from top of Cayo de Tierra

Media Luna

Like the name describes, Media Luna is in the shape of a perfect half moon. This coral sand beach is about a quarter of a mile long bordered by lush coconut palms and sea grapes.

Media Luna is reached by following the road past Sun Bay and then bearing to the left. Continue on that road until you come to the beach.

In general, Media Luna is quieter and less crowded than its immediate neighbor, Sun Bay.

Facilities

Facilities are limited to four small covered pavilions with wooden picnic benches and garbage cans.

Swimming and Snorkeling

A swim area, protected by buoys, extends the length of the beach with the exception of a central dinghy channel. Near shore the sea bottom is sandy, but in the area of the swim buoys and beyond, the bay is covered by a magnificent bed of sea grass, unspoiled so far by turbidity caused by runoff pollution from irresponsible development or damage by anchors and anchor line. Media Luna is well protected against both wind and waves, and as a result, the bay is usually very calm. Additionally, the water is shallow, non threatening and warmer than in deeper bays, making Media Luna an ideal beach for children and beginning swimmers.

Navío Beach

Navío Beach is the last beach that you'll come to on the Sun Bay access road. At the end of Media Luna Beach, bear left and follow the dirt track to Navío. It is a lovely coral sand beach fringed by coconut palms and sea grapes.

Because Navío is the furthest beach on the Sun Bay access road, which is rutted and difficult to negotiate, and because of the wavy condition of the bay, there will usually be less people on Navío than at Sun Bay or Media Luna, and, therefore offering more privacy and peace and quiet. This, in conjunction with the cool and refreshing trade winds, makes Navío Beach ideal for relaxing, picnicking or getting away from it all.

String up a hammock between two palm trees and, in the words of Bob Dylan, "forget about today until tomorrow."

Swimming, Snorkeling and Body Surfing

Navío is exposed to the trade winds and there is usually wind-driven surf that breaks near shore. This wind condition along with the relatively soft sandy bottom of the bay, makes Navío the best beach on Vieques for body surfing and boogie boarding in the summer when there are no breaking waves on the north.

There is excellent snorkeling on both sides of the bay, especially on calm days when you can explore the caves, sea fan beds and colorful sponge and fire coral covered rock walls.

Following a trail that leads west and then turning inland at the first low point, there is narrow path that leads to a salt water pool inside a cave. The pool is fed by an underground passage connecting it to the sea.

For Adventurers

Adventurers who are in good physical shape and have some rock scrambling experience may want to explore the rugged trail that leads to the rocky cliffs between Navío and Media Luna, where a rocky outcropping not far from shore provides a platform for daring jumpers and divers.

Bioluminescent Bay

The August 4, 2008 issue of the Guinness Book of Records declared Puerto Rico's Mosquito Bay in Vieques to be the brightest bio bay in the world.

With the slightest agitation of the water, tiny bioluminescent creatures emit an electric bluish-white light, so that every thing that moves or agitates the water, such as fish, people, boats or raindrops, leave a bioluminescent trail in their wake. This phenomenon of bioluminescence is so intense, so awe-inspiringly beautiful and so dependable that Mosquito Bay in Vieques, also called the Bioluminescent Bay or the Bio Bay, could easily be called the eighth wonder of the world and is something not to be missed if you find yourself on the island.

The organisms responsible for bioluminescence are called dinoflagellates. They can be found in all waters of the ocean as plankton, tiny organisms that live just below the ocean's surface. They have the ability to move via a whip-like tail, but are so small, than in effect they move about at the mercy of the winds, waves, currents and tides.

Special characteristics of certain bays throughout the world create conditions in which dinoflagellates will concentrate and flourish and Mosquito Bay is a perfect example.

The mouth of the bay is situated in such a way that the prevailing winds and currents easily allow ocean water to enter the bay. It is also quite shallow at the entrance so that only the surface waters, which are abundant in plankton, flow into the bay. A relatively narrow channel winds into a large shallow mangrove lagoon downwind from the entrance.

Here, the bioluminescent organisms will concentrate because they can't get out of the bay. They're too small and not fast enough swimmers to find their way upstream snaking through the channel to return to the open ocean. Nor would they want to, because the conditions in the Bio Bay's mangrove lagoon are just right for them.

The entire bay is encircled by mangroves whose leaves are constantly falling into the water. These rotting leaves provide a perfect diet for the dinoflagellates.

Moreover, the salinity of the water is perfectly suitable to the dinoflagellates. It is kept within their narrow tolerance levels because of the presence of lagunas or salt ponds just behind the mangrove lagoon that collect water during periods of high tides and during intense rains and then filter the fresh water back into the bay slowly.

Another important factor is that there is no significant quebrada or fresh water stream leading directly into the Bio Bay that could lower the salinity to drop undesirable levels. Human contamination from sewage, a factor which has seriously degraded a bioluminescent bay on the Big Island, once a rival to Mosquito Bay, is not a problem in Vieques, and hopefully never will be.

Tests have shown that Mosquito Bay contains as many as 720,000 bioluminescent organisms per gallon of water. This concentration is so great that if you splash the water, you will cause them to emit enough light so that you could read the print on a book in the dead of night.

Vieques Travel Journal
August 7, 2003

A Night on the Bio Bay

...at night we went to the Bio Bay with Abe Velásquez. He's been exploring the Bio Bay since he was a kid and he really truly appreciates it.

We put our kayaks in at a beach called Playa de Don Flor that is accessible from the Sun Bay entrance and began to paddle. There was no moon and it was almost totally dark. It was really dark.

That is, if you didn't move.

But we were moving.

And everything and I mean EVERYTHING is glowing and sparkling in electric greenish and bluish-white light. The hulls of the kayaks, the paddles in the water and even the drops of water dripping off the paddles stir up the bioluminescence with little drops of light falling through the air like sparklers on the Fourth of July.

This photo by Frank Borges Llosa shows model, Quisilinda Flores, kayaking on the bio bay. Using a long exposure of the kayak in motion, a flash was set off to make the model brighter on film. The orange glow in the background is from the city lights. The glow has not been manipulated in any way.

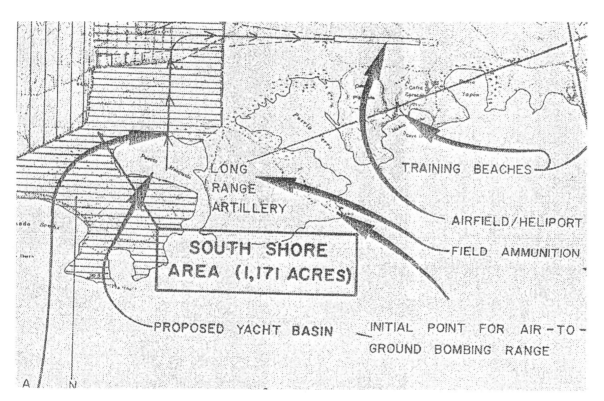

The Navy's Plans for the Bio Bay

In 1969, the Navy presented plans for the development of their eastern lands.

As can be seen on the plans at left their vision for the future destiny of Puerto Mosquito or the Bio Bay was the creation of the following: "PROPOSED YACHT BASIN."

Novilla Beach at the mouth of Bahia Mosquito (Bio Bay)

Playa Negra (Black Sand Beach)

Leaving Esperanza on Route 996, proceed to the intersection of Route 201. Continue west toward La Hueca about 50 yards and look for the Jaguey sign just before the Casa Vieja Art Gallery. On the left (south), below the yellow guard rail is a dry (except in times of very abundant rainfall) riverbed called Quebrada Urbana. Years ago, this quebrada was described by older Viequenses as a flowing river which was rarely dry.

Follow the quebrada through the beautiful dry forest foliage. Along the way, you will see many fruit trees such as mango, tamarind, coconut, papaya and genip. You will find the Black Sand Beach where the quebrada meets the sea, a distance of 0.4 mile (one kilometer). The jet-black sand beach runs to the west for about for a half mile.

Although most of Vieques formed as a result of limestone deposits, some areas, notably Mount Pirata, are volcanic. Some of this volcanic material is a black crystalline substance called magnetite, which washes down the Quebrada Urbana during heavy rains. This magnetite has collected downwind and down current from the mouth of the Quebrada Urbana and has resulted in the only black sand beach in the Virgin Island archipelago.

Magnetite is iron based and, therefore, the black sand on the Black Sand Beach will be attracted to a magnet, a cool science experiment for visiting schoolchildren.

Anibal Corcino and Alicio Ayala, fishermen from Esperanza - *Photo by Ramon Korff*

Fishing

Fishing has been a mainstay cultural activity in the islands of the Caribbean since the days of the first indigenous inhabitants. On Vieques, fishing became even more important because with the loss of the land to the Navy along with the loss of employment on the sugar estates, little else was left for the subsistence of the people. Fishermen were not only providers of food, but also of transportation, and they eventually became cultural leaders in the struggle to stop the Navy bombing on the land and adjacent seas of the island.

Nasas

Nasas are fish traps. In the old days, they were made out of woven vines and West Indian birch braces. Chicken wire siding and steel reinforcement bar (rebar or *varilla*) braces have replaced the old materials.

Single-funneled traps, convex at one end and concave on the other, are traditional for the Puerto Rican and Virgin Islands. In the Lesser Antilles, they are usually larger, rectangular-shaped and have two funnels.

The fish swim in the funnel, which leads to the interior of the trap. The funnel sides extend about half way down to the bottom of the trap. Most fish can't see up; so they can't get out.

The traps are baited, and set at the bottom of the sea in areas adjacent to coral reefs. A line tied to the nasa extends to the surface where it is supported by a buoy. The buoys were carved out of wood in the old days, but now styrofoam is used.

The fishermen leave the trap in the water and haul it every other day. If the line is cut, the trap will be lost.

If the fishermen are ecologically sensitive, a trap door will be cut into the side panel of the trap secured by a biodegradable tie.

This way if the trap is lost, the trap door will prevent the nasa from becoming a death trap, luring more and more fish to their death until the trap deteriorates, which with today's modern materials will be a very long time.

Getting Bait

Bait fish are often caught by throwing a net called an *ataraya* in shallow waters.

Lobsters

In the old days lobsters had no value. If you caught one you would use it for bait to catch fish. When lobsters became commercially viable they were hunted using a torch and a forked stick on the shallow reef at night. You would pin the lobster down with the forked stick and catch it.

Lobsters also can be caught by diving down and getting them out of their holes with a snare, which is a wire noose on the end of a stick. You put the noose over the lobster and then snare it and pull it out of the hole.

Lobsters can also be caught in traps. Although a traditional nasa will also catch lobsters, the rectangular-shaped wooden lobster trap is better for catching lobsters, because the lobsters would rather crawl on wood than on wire. The funnel is on the top and wooden slats extend down about a third of the way into the trap. Lobsters are not as smart as fish and they will hang onto the outside of the trap and let you catch them.

Good bait for lobsters would be something really stinky like an old rotten cow hide (available at the local butcher).

Line Fishing

It seems that on Vieques almost everyone likes to fish. The most popular method is with a good old fashioned rod and reel.

The Puerto Ferro Man

An archeological dig conducted by Luis Chanlatte and Yvonne Narganes in 1990 uncovered the bones of a man who lived there almost 4,000 years ago.

The excavation took place at Puerto Ferro in southern Vieques, a site characterized by huge stone boulders.

The remains and surrounding organic artifacts were dated using carbon dating techniques and studied by forensic scientists.

It is assumed that the Puerto Ferro man, as he is called by archeologists, belonged to one of the first groups of human beings to inhabit Vieques, a pre-ceramic and pre-agricultural people who traveled through the Caribbean islands and survived by hunting, fishing and gathering.

According to the forensic studies, the Puerto Ferro man was about thirty five to forty years old at the time of his death, which was quite an advanced age by the standards of the time. He was also inordinately tall for a man of that period, measuring five foot ten inches in height.

Extensive damage found to the jawbone, which showed no signs of healing, indicates that the cause of death was a strong blow.

Cacimar and Yaureibo

On Vieques, the Taino people lived in relative peace and harmony with their neighbors and their environment for some 1,200 years, until the end of the 15th century when confronted with the arrival of a new people from the other side of the Atlantic Ocean, the Europeans.

Quisqueya (today named Hispaniola, which is made up of Haiti and the Dominican Republic) was the first island to be conquered by the invaders from the east. Boriquén (Puerto Rico) was next. The conquest and subsequent subjugation of the Tainos were unbelievably cruel.

Hundreds of Tainos who lived on the eastern part of Boriquén managed to escape making their way to the nearby Bieké (Vieques), which was as yet unconquered and under the control of two Taino *caciques* (chiefs), the brothers, Yaureibo and Cacimar.

Between 1511 and 1514, the Tainos from Bieké joined the newly arrived refugees in a series of retaliatory raids against the conquerors of Boriquén, a light-skinned people who called themselves Spaniards or Christians.

As a result of the raids, more soldiers were stationed in the eastern zone and fortification and defensive measures were undertaken. One of these soldiers, Sancho de Arango, was the owner of a ferocious dog named Becerrillo (The Little Bull), an animal especially trained to kill human beings.

According to the Chronicle of the Indies:

> The natural instinct of this animal allowed it to distinguish between fugitive Indians or enemy Indians and those that had already been subdued. He attacked his foes with fury and rage and defended his friends with great valor. If a prisoner escaped, Becerrillo would find him no matter where he tried to hide. Among 200 Indians he would seek out and find the one who had fled from his designated job and take him by the arm to the Christians. If he resisted, Becerrillo would tear the man to pieces. The Indians were more afraid of ten Spanish soldiers accompanied by Becerrillo than by 100 soldiers without him.

In 1514, Cacimar led an attack against a Spanish settlement in eastern Boriquén. During the battle, he was run through with a lance from behind as he engaged in hand to hand combat with a Spanish soldier.

Yaureibo, angered by the dishonorable nature of his brother's death, launched a second attack on the settlement. In the battle that ensued, several Spaniards were killed, and many others were wounded. Sancho de Arango, the owner of Becerrillo, was wounded in the battle and taken prisoner along with several of his men.

Becerrillo had been fighting along with the soldiers, but when he saw that his master had been wounded, he furiously attacked the party of warriors who were carrying him away along with several other Spanish captives.

So fierce was the beast's attack, that it caused panic among the warriors who rapidly retreated to the banks of a nearby river, which they hastily crossed.

In the confusion of the retreat, several of the captives were able to escape. A Taino warrior, who had crossed to the other side of the river, managed to kill Becerrillo, piercing him with a poisoned arrow.

It may very well have been the loss of the dog, rather than the loss of Spanish lives, that prompted the Spanish to send a large and well armed force of men to Vieques in order to punish the people there.

Yaureibo and his warriors fought valiantly, holding off the Spanish for an entire night, but in the end the Spaniards with their superior weaponry emerged victorious.

Yaureibo was killed as were many of his people. Many others were captured and sent to Puerto Rico, where they were enslaved.

With the defeat of Yaureibo and Cacimar the era of Viequense self determination came to an end and the people of Vieques became pawns in a game of colonialism that some feel continues to this very day.

Taino Zemis

El Este - The East

The Eastern Lands

The lands on the eastern end of Vieques were expropriated by the US Navy during the 1940s and 1950s. The former farmlands, lagoons, mangrove forests and beaches including the humble abodes and properties of Viequense *campesinos* became the Inner Range of the Atlantic Fleet Weapons Training Facility (AFWTF).

This was divided into the Eastern Maneuver Area (EMA), the Surface Impact Range (SIA) and the Live Impact Area (LIA).

The EMA was used for such activities as a small arms range, practice minefields, electronic warfare and mock amphibious assaults.

The SIA was used for practice shelling from ground artillery positions and from warships offshore.

The LIA was the target for the really big stuff, bombs dropped from jet aircraft, missiles fired from ships and planes and for the testing of an assortment of both conventional and non conventional weapons. Non-conventional usually refers to nuclear, chemical and biological weapons. Non-conventional weapons tested on Vieques that the public knows about include depleted uranium artillery shells, Agent Orange, napalm, chaff (an aluminum coated fiberglass dust that serves to form a cloud impenetrable to radar) and in 1966, a "test bomb with nuclear characteristics" that was meant to be tested on the Vieques range, but was accidentally dropped in the sea between St. Thomas and Vieques. (The bomb was recovered at great expense by a crack team of divers aided by dolphins from the Navy's then super secret animal research laboratory.)

In addition to the land areas on Vieques, the surrounding waters, which the Navy called the "Outer Range," were used for an assortment of bombing, missile and artillery exercises.

How did the Viequenses Benefit From the Navy Base?

Until the closing of the Marine base in the 1970s, Camp Garcia housed about 300 Marines on a semi permanent basis.

The "Navy Base" on Vieques, however, was not really a base at all in the traditional sense of the word. Vieques was a target; a target for use by the US military and available for rent to foreign nations. In military parlance, it was a "stand-alone" bombing range, in that it was located outside of the supporting Navy base, which was Roosevelt Roads, located on the Big Island.

There were no parade grounds, no major facilities for the housing of a semi-permanent community of officers and enlisted men who would stay on the island, contributing to the economy. In short, aside from a few menial jobs in maintenance and security, Vieques didn't benefit at all.

> "I think that obviously there's a recognition that there are clear needs; consideration that the people of Vieques deserve; if you compare the situation of Vieques to other training locations -- say, in the continental United States, you'll find that the people of Vieques have for a number of years borne the burdens of hosting a training range without many of the rewards. If you compare that to training ranges around bases here in the United States, for example, you'll find that these states host a large number of troops. These troops live in the community. They buy cars at the local dealerships. They eat at the local restaurants. They go to the local schools. That draws impact aid to those communities so that there's a clear benefit to having a base in your state. The people of Vieques do not host the same volume of Navy personnel."
>
> *Mr. P.J. Crowley, Navy public relations officer, at the Pentagon news briefing for President Clinton's January directives on Vieques.*

Painting by Sandra Reyes

Wildlife Preserve

On May 1, 2003, the former Navy controlled lands of eastern Vieques were transferred from the US Department of the Navy to the US Department of the Interior to be managed by the US Department of Fish and Wildlife as a Wildlife Preserve, making Vieques the home of the largest Wildlife Preserve in the Caribbean.

The 900 acres in the former Live Impact Area will be managed as a "Wilderness Area" where all public access is prohibited. (Paradoxically, the Wilderness Act defines 'Wilderness Areas' as places "where the earth and its community of life are untrammeled by man.")

Public access is also prohibited to the majority of the Wildlife Refuge as well.

According to the Department of Fish and Wildlife, the former Navy bombing range and training facilities on Vieques have been designated as a National Wildlife Refuge because "in ecological terms, parts of the island are very valuable, Vieques has one of the best dry sub-tropical forests in the Caribbean and it is home to at least four endangered plant species and ten endangered animal species."

Oscar Díaz, a previous manager of the Wildlife Refuge, explained that as long as the Department of Fish and Wildlife is responsible for these lands, they will remain committed to the preservation of the natural environments of Vieques, environments that have all but disappeared through overdevelopment on the Big Island and throughout much of the Caribbean.

Nonetheless, many Viequenses feel that the designation of the former Navy-controlled lands as a Wildlife Refuge, will limit the scope and timeliness of the promised clean up of these lands by the Navy.

Many also feel that on Vieques, where the cancer rate is 27% higher than on the Big Island, the continued presence of depleted uranium dust, explosive residues, heavy metals and other possible contaminants not yet revealed is the cause of many of the serious health problems effecting the people of the island.

Photo Courtesy of the Department of Fish & Wildlife

Vieques Times July 2003 Issue - Volume 149

Navy Out...Wildlife In

Most people agreed: It was good to get the bombing stopped.

...So you won, you got what you wanted...

Haven't won yet. All we got was a change of uniforms. The fence is still there, the guards are still there, with the guns and the bullet-proof vests - and the biggest chunk of Vieques is still off limits to the people of Vieques. Even if they let us in to one of the beaches, we can't stay to watch the sunset, they throw us out before six, carloads of armed guards... What's this all about?

So how does this play on the island.

In a blatant generalization we observe that:

The English-speaking sector is tickled pink with the FWS presence.

Fish and Wildlife is a Federal agency, not Puerto Rican. They will protect us from Puerto Rican squatters and off-island developers. And the largest Wildlife Refuge in the Caribbean looks great in the tourism brochures.

The mainstream Spanish-speaking sector and the scientific community are concerned that:

The Wildlife Refuge and the fenced-off Wilderness Refuge designation will provide the Navy with a cop-out for limited cleanup. The decontamination policy could be less stringent for an unpopulated area as opposed to a zone suitable for human habitation. The fear is that toxic contaminants left in the ground will (and do) migrate to the civilian sector.

The landless:

See vast tracts reserved for lizards and rodents and little hope to find land on which to build a home for their families.

The political activists:

See Fish and Wildlife Service as trustees for the Navy estate. They warn that the Navy could be simply cooling its heels somewhere backstage awaiting the cue to come storming back.

FWS is working with Navy funds and has hired the same civilian (armed) guards the Navy used for patrols (and often for informers). A protest movement against FWS is already forming.

Access to the Wildlife Refuge

Until 1999, when a 500-pound bomb exploded in an observation area and killed security guard, David Sanes, most of Camp Garcia was open to the public, including the beaches of the north shore such as Puerto Negro and Playa Violeta. Protest demonstrations following the Sanes incident led the Navy to close all of the camp to the public.

Public Access is now limited to the eastern shore of Bahía Puerto Ferro, Playa Caracas, and Playa de la Chiva.

Within the area where public access is permitted, certain areas, such as the site of the old airport, the former camp area and several other sites, are also off limits to the public.

The restricted areas are those that have not been certified as safe by the US Navy and may contain unexploded ordnance (UXO), munitions and explosives of concern (MEC) or other dangerous substances.

The restricted areas are well marked and roads leading into these prohibited zones are blocked off with gates. The preserve is accessible from 6:00 A.M. to 6:00 P.M., at which time it is mandatory that you leave the area.

Activities such as hunting, catching land crabs, camping and lighting campfires are prohibited.

Accessible Areas

Notwithstanding these limitations, the relatively small area open to the public contains beautiful beaches, miles of dirt roads suitable for hiking, horseback riding, mountain biking and four-wheel drive exploration.

There are also small secluded bays and rocky shorelines from where you can swim, kayak, snorkel or fish as well as caves, blowholes, salt ponds, quebradas, mangrove forests and magnificent vistas from the tops of sheer cliffs.

Searching for unexploded ordenance with metal detectors and bomb-sniffing dogs.

Photo Courtesy of US Fish & Wildlife

Photo by Steve Simonsen

Puerto Diablo

Some of the very best beaches in Vieques lie in the restricted area where public access is denied. The photo on the left shows two beaches in the former Puerto Diablo Barrio in Eastern Vieques.

Puerto Diablo (Devil's Bay) is considered to be the southern tip of the mysterious Devil's Triangle. This refers to an area of the Atlantic Ocean lying roughly between Miami, Florida, Hamilton, Bermuda and Puerto Diablo, Vieques. The Devil's Triangle is notorious as an area where an inordinate number of aircraft and ocean vessels have disappeared without a trace.

"Yellow Beach" Photo Courtesy of US Department of Fish & Wildlife

Naming Vieques Beaches

The largest and most popular accessible beaches in Camp Garcia are Caracas in Bahía Corcho (Red Beach), Manuelquí in Bahía de la Chiva (Blue Beach), and Playuela.

Many of the beaches in Vieques were renamed after colors, such as Red, Blue, Green and Purple.

These beaches were used by the Navy to practice amphibious landings and it was through these practice operations that the beaches got their new names.

In a simulation of war, Marines would leave their bases on Navy ships headed for Vieques. They would be briefed as to what was expected of them.

"Never leave the group. Stay with your buddy. Beware of poisonous snakes. Do not make contact with the dangerous natives."

They were not told where they were going. They were just to make the landing and establish their position on the beach.

As the ships approached Vieques, reconnaissance teams would disembark and surreptitiously land on the beaches, where, among other activities, they would raise large colored banners on the beaches. These banners would indicate which beach a team would assault.

Those assigned to Bahía Corcho would assault the beach with the red flags. Those to Bahía de la Chiva would assault the beach with the blue flags and so on. The names stuck and most tourists and North American expatriates, as well as many Viequenses, referred to these beaches by their Navy assigned names.

Now with the Navy gone, signs have been changed and it is hoped that the beaches will again be called by their original names and that the color designations of the beaches will fall into the category of historical curiosities.

Playa Caracas "Red Beach"

When not being used for amphibious assault practice, beautiful Playa Caracas was the choice beach for officers' recreation. It was reopened to the public on May 1, 2003 and is now a local's favorite.

Like many of the beaches, bays and other places on Vieques, Playa Caracas is known by several names.

The name Caracas comes from its location in front of the hill, Cerro Caracas. It is also known as Corcho or Bahía Corcho because it lies within the bay, Bahía Corcho. The Navy called it Red Beach.

Enter through the Camp Garcia gate on Route 997. Proceed 1.7 miles where there is an informational sign. Turn right. Playa Caracas is at the end of the road about three quarters of a mile from the sign.

Manuelquí (Playa de la Chiva) "Blue Beach"

Most military experts agree that in modern warfare, the casualties involved in landing troops on a fortified enemy beach would be too high to be acceptable. Today, Marines are taken to their objective in helicopters, which can arrive from 200-300 miles away. Although practicing amphibious assaults has been called "as obsolete as practicing cavalry charges," it was one of the most commonly practiced military maneuvers on Vieques.

Manuelquí possesses the ideal conditions for amphibious landings and was the Navy's favorite beach to conduct these activities. It is a long stretch of sandy beach within a large protected bay. The sand slopes gradually into the sea and is not so soft as to bog down vehicles exiting landing craft.

Navy warships would lay offshore disgorging men and materiel onto amphibious landing craft. The Marines would land on the beach with weapons blazing, firing at imaginary enemies. Although the military value of this maneuver was questionable, it was exciting and realistic; so much so that on almost every such maneuver, Hollywood filmmakers were on hand to film the action. If you go to the movies and see scenes of US Marines landing on some beach in the Pacific, chances are it was filmed in Vieques on Manuelquí.

Today with the Navy gone, the same characteristics that made Manuelquí perfect for amphibious landings make it perfect for swimming, snorkeling, picnicking and relaxing.

Manuelquí

Manuelquí (*Cayo Manuel or Manuel Cay*) is named after a man named Manuel who lived on the island that lies just off the beach called Cayo de la Chiva.

Manuelquí is also known as Playa de la Chiva because of its location within the Bahía de la Chiva. The beach has also been called Cayo Pepsi Cola.

When the Navy took over the eastern lands they renamed Manuelquí as they did most of the other beaches under their control. Manuelquí became Blue Beach.

There are actually three separate beaches inside the bay separated by small rocky points of land.

To get to Manuelquí, turn into the former Camp Garcia compound on Route 997. Proceed 1.7 miles where there will be an informational sign on your right. Don't turn; just continue on the same track.

About one mile from the sign the road forks; bear right. The first entrance to Manuelquí will be just a little more than one mile away. To reach the eastern sections of the beach, continue on the same road. You will come to an iron bridge that crosses a quebrada, which leads to a laguna (salt pond) on your left.

For the next mile or so, all of the roads that go off to your right will lead to some section of one of Manuelquí's beaches.

Playuela
"Garcia Beach"

There are two beaches within Bahía Corcho. Caracas on the east and Playuela on the west.

Enter through the Camp Garcia gate on Route 997. Proceed 1.7 miles where there is an informational sign. Turn right. Take the second right turn, which will be about a half mile from the sign. (The first right goes to the old Navy airfield.) Make the next left turn and Playuela will be at the end of the road.

Playuela is somewhat exposed to the easterly trades, so when the breezes are blowing, Playuela can offer some decent bodysurfing.

Playuela has no formal facilities, but it is an excellent hammock and picnic beach. Not that all the other Vieques beaches aren't suitable for these activities, but Playuela is especially good, because of the convenient palm and sea grape trees, the availability of shade under these trees, and the comparative isolation of the beach.

Photo by Ramon Korff

The Beginning of the Fishermen's War
A Practice Amphibious Landing on Bahía de la Chiva That Never Happened
from a conversation with Carlos (Taso) Zenón

In 1975, the fishermen of Vieques formed the Vieques Fishermen's Association. The group was not created to oppose the presence of the US Navy in Vieques, but rather to address more immediate problems such as the lack of a dock and a proper location to clean, process and sell fish.

Most fishermen in Vieques used fish traps as a mainstay of their art. The traps, locally called nasas, are made of chicken wire and reinforced with saltwater-resistant wooden sticks cut from local trees. They are generally set in 60 to 150 feet of water and are attached to a line, which leads to a floating buoy about one foot in diameter. The traps are hauled by hand about once every two days.

A major problem for the Viequense fishermen was that the large naval ships were running over the fish trap buoys and cutting the line leading to the traps. When this happens, the traps, which represent a good deal of time and money to the fishermen, are lost forever.

One night in 1977, 131 fish trap buoys were cut.

It was at this juncture that the Vieques Fishermen's Association entered the political arena. The Association brought a lawsuit against the United States Navy for the loss of these traps. Hoping to squash the case before it went to trial, the Navy asked for, and was granted, a change of venue, so that the trial would be heard in Virginia instead of Puerto Rico. This was a severe problem for the fishermen, who lived simply and did not have money for such luxuries as airlines and travel expenses.

Nonetheless, the fishermen were able to get together the airfare and sent a delegation including the president of the Association, Carlos (Taso) Zenón. They found lodging in the cheapest of motels, ate as economically as possible, and to the surprise of Navy attorneys, appeared at court.

At the hearing, the judge was sympathetic to the fishermen. He admonished the Navy lawyers for their tactic of forcing the poor fishermen who he knew had little money and who spoke Spanish to travel to the mainland United States to appear in court. The judge found for the fishermen and the Navy had to reimburse them for the lost fish traps.

The fishermen were emboldened. It was their first real victory against the Navy. In February of 1978, the Navy announced that 20 member nations of the North Atlantic Treaty Organization (NATO) would be conducting maneuvers in and around Vieques for 28 days and that during that time no fishing boats would be allowed to leave port.

In response, Taso and a delegation of fishermen traveled to the Roosevelt Roads Naval Base on the Big Island and met with the Admiral in charge, William Flanagan. During the meeting it was explained that a 28-day moratorium on fishing would deal a devastating blow to the fishermen. They had no other means of support and they would not be able to provide for the needs of their families.

The Admiral's response was that the fishermen should apply for food stamps. Taso looked the Admiral in the eye and said, "You don't know my people. You are going to have problems."

The delegation returned to Vieques and called an emergency meeting of the Fishermen's Association. Taso told the assembly that Admiral Flanagan suggested that they could all line up for food stamps at the welfare office.

The expression on the faces of the fishermen clearly expressed how they felt about giving up fishing and collecting welfare instead. Then Taso announced, "We are going to fight."

One of the fishermen asked exactly how they could fight against the battleships, helicopters and planes of the NATO forces. Nonetheless, the fishermen came up with a plan.

The Navy announced to the press that the NATO exercises would begin with an amphibious landing at Bahía de la Chiva where 2,500 fully armed Marines would be brought ashore in less than 45 minutes.

The fishermen made their own announcement. They told the media that the Vieques Fishermen's Association was not going to allow even one Marine to land on Bahía de la Chiva that day.

The newspaper and media people were intrigued. They sent reporters and photographers from major newspapers and television and radio syndications to be on hand to document the confrontation.

On the morning of the planned amphibious assault, 18 fishing boats left Esperanza en route to Bahía de la Chiva. Each boat had two men aboard. In addition, two larger boats carrying the reporters and photographers from the news media joined the flotilla.

The two opposing forces met just offshore from the idyllic tropical beach known to the Viequenses as Bahía de la Chiva and to the Navy as Blue Beach. On one side were the giant warships of the NATO superpowers, and on the other, the small open wooden fishing boats of the Viequense fishermen.

The image of the Navy boats running over the fish trap buoys and cutting the lines with their propellers may have inspired the fishermen's strategy, because each of their boats carried aboard a fish trap buoy attached to a line, except that this time the line did not have a fish trap at the other end. It had a length of heavy iron chain. At a signal from the commanding officer, the Marines climbed down rope ladders onto amphibious landing craft which, one by one proceeded at full throttle toward the beach.

A Viequense fishing boat sped toward the first approaching amphibious landing craft as if it was going to crash into the large vessel head on. At the last minute, the Viequense captain deftly maneuvered his little boat so that it veered off passing just to one side of the bow of Navy boat.

The other fisherman aboard then threw the fish trap buoy into the water. Then the captain turned the little boat around in a tight circle and sped in front of the oncoming landing craft. Meanwhile, the other fisherman let out the line until he was left holding only the chain. At this point, the captain stopped the boat and the two fishermen waited. When the line handler on the little boat felt the tug of the line getting caught in the assault craft's propeller, (something like the feel of a big fish hitting a hook, I suppose) he let go of the chain. Then the inevitable happened. The line wrapped around the propeller shaft until the heavy chain was sucked into the propeller.

Bang! The first assault craft was put out of action.

The second landing craft met the same fate and then the third, fourth, fifth, sixth, seventh, eighth, ninth and tenth. They were all stopped dead in their tracks.

Meanwhile, the Admiral, forced to accept the superior military strategy of the Viequense fishermen, called a halt to the exercise and just as Taso had declared to the press, not one Marine had landed on Bahía de la Chiva that morning.

Photo by Ramon Korff

Civil Disobedience Camps on Cayo Yayi - Photo by Steve Simonsen

The Civil Disobedience Camps

On April 19, 1999, the pilot of an FA 18 fighter jet practicing bombing maneuvers on Vieques missed the target zone and dropped a 500-pound bomb in the vicinity of the an observation post (OP 1), killing Viequense security guard, David Sanes and injuring four others.

The community was outraged and members of the Committee for the Rescue and Development of Vieques and local fishermen organized a combination memorial service and civil disobedience action.

Among the demonstrators was the environmentalist, Alberto de Jesus, better known as Tito Kayak. True to his nickname and symbolic of the Vieques struggle, Tito Kayak had paddled his kayak all the way from the Big Island in order to arrive in Vieques and take part in the protest demonstration, a lone seafarer in a tiny craft on his way to confront the giant warships of the world's most powerful Navy.

Tito Kayak was already well known for his high profile acts of civil disobedience. He had paddled over to a Navy warship and, while TV cameras were rolling and sailors on deck were attempting to upset his kayak with high pressure fire hoses, succeeded in painting his "Peace for Vieques" message in large red letters on the hull of the battleship.

In San Juan, Tito Kayak had placed a large banner on top of a 150-foot-high scaffold near the Plaza Las Americas shopping center reading "No to Plutonium" to protest the voyage of the vessel Pacific Swan that was scheduled to transport a cargo of the highly radioactive metal, plutonium, through the Mona Passage, the channel that separates Puerto Rico from Hispaniola.

Perhaps, Tito's best known act of civil disobedience occurred in New York City in November of 2000. Braving high winds and the almost certainty of arrest, he slipped out a window inside the Statue of Liberty, climbed up on the crown and unfurled the Puerto Rican and Vieques flags, along with a banner which read, Paz Para Vieques. Running out of line with which to tie the last part of the banner, he called to his friends who were inside to take the laces off of his sneakers so he would be able to finish the job.

Two days after the errant missile took the life of David Sanes, protesters boarded fishing boats at the dock in Esperanza and were taken to the bombing range. Once there, they planned to participate in a quiet ceremony of prayer, place a giant cross on the mountain near where David Sanes was killed and then return to Esperanza.

Things did not go entirely as planned. Tito Kayak announced that he intended to stay on the bombing range, protect the memorial crucifix and act as a human shield to stop the bombing. His words to his fellow protesters later became the rallying cry of the struggle, *ni una bomba más.* (Not one more bomb.)

The organizers of the demonstration had not anticipated this turn of events. Tito Kayak's independent action was bucking the established order of things, whereby tactics were discussed and voted on by committee members.

The protest organizers asked Tito Kayak to reconsider. He refused. The demonstrators then returned to the beach, boarded the waiting yolas and motored back downwind to Esperanza. Tito Kayak remained on the range, alone.

The next morning, one of Carlos and Eleida Zenón's sons, Cacimar Zenón, brought food, water and supplies to Tito Kayak and decided to stay on the bombing range along with Tito. The next day, Pablo Connelly, the son of Charlie Connelly and Myrna Pagán, editors of *The Vieques Times*, joined the two courageous young men on the range, an area littered with unexploded ordnance and contaminated by heavy metals, depleted uranium and other toxic substances.

Pablo Connelly, addressing a group of visitors to the camps said, "I know that there is a great danger. I know that the risks are great, but all the risks are worth it. I do this for my children and for the children of all Viequenses and I know that during the time that I remain here not a single bomb will fall on Vieques."

Over the course of the following year, what was once considered a provocative and crazy idea became mainstream thinking among activists opposed to the Navy presence on Vieques. In addition to the original camp, known as Monte David, more than one dozen other groups set up camps on the bombing range, including Rubén Berríos of the Puerto Rico Independence Party (PIP), schoolteachers, labor unions, religious groups and other organizations. Supporters arrived daily from the Big Island, from the United States mainland and from abroad. Many well known public figures such as Hillary Clinton, Jesse Jackson, the Governor of New York, George Pataki, the Dalai Lama, actors Martin Sheen and Edward James Olmos and singers Jose Feliciano and Ricky Martin publicly expressed their solidarity with the protesters.

This resolve, of "not one more bomb" was shared by not only the vast majority of the population of Vieques but also by the people of Puerto Rico, the religious establishment and by all the Puerto Rican political parties, at least for a while.

On January 31, 2000, President Clinton issued a directive, which would allow the Navy to continue their training exercises on Vieques until May 1, 2003. By the terms of the directive, a referendum would take place in a year's time whereby the citizens of Vieques could choose either to accept the three years of bombing or to allow indefinite naval exercises on the island. Vieques would be given $40 million in aid. If they chose to allow the Navy to remain on the island, an additional $50 million would be allotted. The directive also promised to return 8,200 acres of land in the western portion of the island to the municipality on December 31, 2000.

(Congress changed the directive and the result was that 4,000 acres were returned to the municipality on May 1, 2001. Three thousand one hundred acres were turned over to the Department of the Interior to be managed by the Department of Fish and Wildlife as a Wildlife Preserve, 700 acres were given to the Puerto Rico Department of Natural Resources and 200 acres (the ROTHR site and the radar installation at the top of Mount Pirata were kept by the Navy.)

The referendum did not include the choice of an immediate withdrawal of the Navy from Vieques, and was soundly rejected by protest organizations and the Puerto Rican churches.

> "Never again shall we tolerate abuse which no community in any of the fifty states would ever be asked to tolerate. We, the people of Puerto Rico, have graduated from colonial passivity, Ni una bomba más. Never again shall we tolerate such abuse. Not for sixty years...and not for sixty minutes."
>
> *Puerto Rico Governor Pedro Rosselló before the Senate Armed Services Committee October 19, 1999*

Despite his having so emphatically endorsed the "no more bombs" policy, Governor Rosselló later changed his position and signed the agreement.

Taso Zenón and his sons, Cacimar y Pedro, en el Campamento Monte David
Photo Courtesy of the Zenón Family

Religious leaders in Puerto Rico organized what turned out to be the largest mass demonstration in the history of Puerto Rico in opposition to the Governor's authorization of the directive.

On May 4, 2000, at the break of dawn, helicopters bearing heavily armed Federal Marshals landed in the impact zone. The occupants of the camps were apprehended, handcuffed, and carried away. Their camps were razed to make way for a new wave of bombing. Many protesters served time in prison, including several important public figures. Environmental lawyer Robert F. Kennedy Jr. was sentenced to 30 days in prison for trespassing. The Reverend Al Sharpton was also arrested for trespassing and given a 90-day prison sentence.

Jacqueline Jackson, the wife of the Rev. Jesse Jackson, spent 10 days in jail for protesting on Vieques. Puerto Rican Senator Norma Burgos was sentenced to 40 days in jail, but when she suggested that the judge put the Navy on trial instead of the demonstrators, the judge added 20 days to her sentence.

New York City Councilman Adolfo Carrión, Bronx Democratic Chairman Roberto Ramirez and New York State Assemblyman José Rivera, were sentenced to 40 days in prison. New York union leader Dennis Rivera was given 30 days.

Puerto Rico Independence Party President, Rubén Berríos, was sentenced to four months in jail as was Dámaso Serrano, the mayor of Vieques.

Actor, Edward James Olmos and U.S. Representative, Luis Gutierrez of Illinois and many other protesters also suffered arrests and served time in jail.

In June of 2001, US President George W. Bush announced the end of military maneuvers on Vieques beginning May 1, 2003. The referendum, the outcome of which would have certainly been against further bombing, was cancelled.

targets on live impact area

Coconut Palms

The coconut palms on the western end of Bahía de la Chiva are some of the few left on the beach. In the past, the beach was lined with beautiful coconut palms, the icon of the Caribbean. The palms, however, were cut down by Marines for war games.

In a 1950s war game, Brigadier General W.W. Harris in charge of the 65th U.S. Infantry was charged with defending the island in a mock battle. In order to prevent the opposing side from making an easy landing, he needed to establish beach fortifications and obstacles. In his book *Puerto Rico's Fighting 65th Infantry*, he explains how he accomplished this goal.

Observing that the coconut palms alongside the beach grew in a dense thicket extending some 100 yards inland from the beach, the General decided to make use of them to defend the beach. He then had his men cut down the palms and enmesh the fallen trees with barb wire and mock demolitions.

It was a brilliant defense and largely through this tactic the 65th infantry won the battle. The opposing team was stopped in their tracks, when they tried to land on the beach. The umpires charged with assessing the damage attributed a 40% casualty rate to the attacking forces and the games had to await the clearing of the obstacles before they could continue.

Cleaning up the mess was no easy task. An entire division of well equipped Marines had not been able to cut their way through. In the end, tanks were used to drag the debris away, and the war games were able to continue.

So much for the palm trees, however.

On October 12, 2003, participants in "The Second Rally for Peace" planted 100 coconut palms at Playa de la Chiva.

Second Rally For Peace
On October 12, 2003, demonstrators marched from the Camp garcia gate to the eastern end of Playa de la Chiva, which is as far as you can legally go in the new Vieques Wildlife Refuge.

Community Activists Demands

Activists on Vieques have summarized their demands as the four D's: *Desmilitarización, Descontaminación, Devolución and Desarrollo Sustentable.* (Demilitarization, Decontamination, Return of the Land and Sustainable Development.)

As of May 1, 2003, the first goal, Demilitarization was achieved. The other three D's, however, remain as issues on the island.

Decontamination

Activists are pressing for a timely and effective cleanup of the land, claiming that the continued presence of heavy metals, depleted uranium and other toxic explosive residues jeopardize the health of Vieques residents.

Return of the Lands (Devolución)

Activists feel that the lands expropriated by the Navy rightfully belongs to the Viequenses and should be returned.

Sustainable Development (Desarrollo Sustentable)

Activists would like to avoid the unrestricted development that they have seen on other Caribbean islands. They would rather promote a sustainable economy emphasizing such activities as eco-tourism, agriculture, fishing, marine biology and archeology. They also are pressing for government controls on the massive land speculation that has followed the exodus of the Navy and has caused prices to skyrocket, putting homes and property out of the reach of the average Viequense family.

Detoxification

But there are many in the community effected by the presence of heavy metals in their bodies who feel that there is a fifth "D," which must be realized before they can enjoy their right to good health and the pursuit of happiness and without which none of the other D's can be enjoyed: Detoxification.

Bibliography

Bernache-Baker, Barbara; *The Bioluminescent Bays of Vieques,* 1995

Chanlatte Baik, Luis A.; *Cultura Ostionoide: Un Desarrollo Agroalfarero Antillano,* San Juan, Puerto Rico, 1986

Cordero Ventura, Cruz; *Vieques, Sesenta Años de Bombardeos en Tiempos de Paz*, 2001

Grupo de Apoyo Técnico y Profesional Para el Desarrollo Sustenable de Vieques; *Guías Para el Desarrollo Sustenable de Vieques,* 2002

Harris, Brigadier General W.W.; *Puerto Rico's Fighting 65th Infantry,* Presidio Press, Novato CA, 1980

La Cultura Saladoide en Puerto Rico, Museo de Historia, Anthropología y Arte, Universidad de Puerto Rico, Rio Piedras, Puerto Rico, 2002

McCaffrey, Katherine T.; *Military Power and Popular Protest*, Rutgers University Press, New Brunswick, NJ

Meléndez Lopez, Auturo; *La Batalla de Vieques*, Editorial Edil, Rio Piedras, Puerto Rico, 2000

Pagán, Tere Villegas; *Taso, Un Pedazo de Vieques,* 2002

Ruiz, J. Pastor; *Vieques Antiguo y Moderno,* 1947